Supporting the Child of Exceptional Ability

At Home and School

Second Edition

Susan Leyden

David Fulton Publishers
London

in association with

The National Association for Able Children in Education

David Fulton Publishers Ltd
Ormond House, 26–27 Boswell Street, London WC1N 3JD

First published in Great Britain by David Fulton Publishers 1998

Note: The right of Susan Leyden to be identified as the author of this work has been asserted by her in accordance with the Copyright, Designs and Patents Act 1988.

British Library Cataloguing in Publication Data
A catalogue record for this book is available from the British Library

ISBN 1–85346–516–X

Typeset by Textype Ltd, Cambridge
Printed in Great Britain by The Cromwell Press Ltd, Trowbridge, Wilts.

Contents

Preface

Andrew began reading at 14 months. His mother said she had to ration his reading by the time he was three, so that it would remain a pleasure. By the time he entered school at five Andrew was showing quite unusual ability, not only in the area of language (he had gone some way to learning a number of foreign languages through reading 'phrase' books) but also in music and mathematics. A tape-recording of him reading one of his stories to the village school-teacher reveals a richness of imagination and wit that would be quite extraordinary in any child. In a child of five it is almost alarming. Two years later the child can be heard explaining how he had transcribed music from tunes he heard on television, by working out the 'key signatures', the rhythms and the correct notation. He then moves on to problem solving using a slide rule: 'Set X to D, 3, 5, C line to X. Under the 25 on C read the answer 875 on D. Rough check 4 times the product times 2 equals 8. So answer is 8.75.'

Andrew was a brilliant child. No-one was in any doubt about that. No-one, either, believed that meeting the teaching and social needs of such a child would be easy. Children as extraordinary as Andrew are, by definition, very rare. Many of us will not meet one in our lifetime. If we do, we are likely to acknowledge the very real and special needs they will have, and we are also likely to want to help them. What we are perhaps less ready to acknowledge is that among our children in school there will be many other children with exceptional abilities such as Anthony, Fiona, Martin and Joanna whom we meet in this book. There are far more than we realise. Some will have been welcomed and encouraged to develop their talents to the full. Others may have been acknowledged, but their exceptional intelligence may not have made them many friends. And yet others, far too many others, will have found ways of deliberately or subconsciously suppressing or diverting their natural abilities because of social pressures to conform.

It cannot be right to accept situations where children find it necessary to dampen down their intellectual energy, or where they are discouraged from declaring their justifiable frustration. Our business as parents and teachers must be to create appropriate and helpful environments for children, to create climates in which positive attitudes to themselves and to others can be developed, and in which excitement and enthusiasm for learning can be shared.

Public interest in the care and education of exceptionally able children tends to wax and wane according to current political and economic concerns. Whether or not such interest is topical or fashionable at any given time, the fact remains that exceptionally able children exist. They live within their families; they attend our schools; they are loved and cared for by their parents; and they are taught and guided by their teachers. Parents and teachers are not primarily concerned whether there is a national interest in certain labelled groups of children. They are concerned with individuals, with the child they know, and for whom they strive to do their best to promote a healthy and happy development. Exceptionally able children are first and foremost *children*. Their need for love, understanding and acceptance is as great as that of any other child. Love may be readily available to them. Understanding and acceptance may prove more difficult.

This book is about the growth of relationships, with particular regard to the consequences of exceptional development. It offers a perspective on the development of children who have exceptional abilities and discusses how, through a better understanding of their needs, we might all contribute to improving their learning environments. Issues which emerge at the various stages of a child's growth from early infancy to adolescence are examined from theoretical and practical viewpoints. It is not a manual of guidance for either parents or teachers, though approaches to making provision in school and ways of structuring the curriculum are discussed in the relevant chapters. For more detailed advice the reader is advised to consult one of the many excellent texts now on the market listed in the bibliography section.

The picture presented here is a personal one and has been developed as a result of many years working with a great number of pupils, parents and teachers, and listening to children describe their experiences. The interpretation owes much to the author's own search for understanding about the growth of self-knowledge and the management of relationships. The approach is based on a belief that the many problems that face young people, their families and their schools require insights rather than prescription. A problem recognised and shared is halfway to a problem solved.

All children described are based on actual case studies of children I have met and with whom I have worked, though the names and some details have been changed in the interests of maintaining confidentiality. The convention for using masculine or feminine pronouns always presents a dilemma when writing about children in general. There is the risk of causing offence, whichever pronoun is chosen, and it is unwieldy to combine the two by using him and her, and s/he. I have chosen to vary their use from chapter to chapter.

The book could not have been written without encouragement and support from many people with whom I have worked over the years. I am grateful to Marvin Close for his witty cartoons which bring a life and a lightness to the text and prevent it from being altogether too serious, to Stuart Harrison and the children of Hempsill Hall school for some of the photographs, to Ruth Larbey for her poem, to Gwen Goodhew for examples of teacher planning, and to Gervase Leyden for his unstinting support and patience, and helpful comment. Above all, thanks must be due to all the many children and their parents, whose generosity and willingness to share their experience has developed my own understanding.

Susan Leyden
Gibsmere, Notts
1998

The National Association for Able Children in Education
Westminster College, Oxford OX2 9AT

The Association that Helps Teachers Help Able and Talented Children

AIMS

- To raise awareness of the particular educational needs which able and talented children have, in order to realise their full potential.

- To be proactive in promoting discussion and debate by raising relevant issues through liaison with educational policy makers.

- To ensure a broad, balanced and appropriate curriculum for able and talented children.

- To advocate the use of a differentiated educational provision in the classroom through curriculum enrichment and extension.

- To encourage commitment to the personal, social and intellectual development of the whole child.

- To make education an enjoyable, exciting and worthwhile experience for the able and talented.

Chapter 1

Introduction: beyond normal expectations

Katie was a startlingly pretty child with a mass of auburn curls, huge blue eyes, and dimples. She sang with a true, clear voice, took dancing and guitar lessons, and enjoyed writing stories. She was an avid reader. She was also an outgoing child, very much at ease in the company of adults whom she liked to entertain with bright social conversation. She was confident in manner, even a little gracious. Her parents adored her; I disliked her on sight. For Katie was only three years old. Poor Katie.

Apart from her doting parents, no-one felt comfortable in her presence. Everything about her jarred one's expectations.

First there was the contrast within the family. Both parents were in their late 40s when Katie was born, and were usually taken to be her grandparents. Then there was the mismatch between her age and the manner and content of her conversation. The unexpectedness of it, the discomfort of being addressed in such adult terms by such a tiny child aroused a sense of indignation and disapproval in those who met her. On top of all this were the surprising accomplishments. A three-year-old is just not expected to be able to do all the things that she did, and with such evident enthusiasm. Katie was something discordant. She was an exceptional child – and no-one liked her.

Anthony was another unusual child. A friend came to tea bringing with him Anthony, his nine-year-old son. Seated round the table we talked of this and that, of mundane affairs, ordinary concerns, until someone asked the boy about his interest in some science project. From an awkward and rather taciturn lad, he became transformed: his eyes lit up, his hands moved rapidly in the air, words poured forth, theories were expounded, experiments explained in lengthy and (for us) confusing detail, references made which were beyond the under-standing and experience of any others present. We listened with mounting feelings of amazement and dismay. I remember thinking that we were hearing something remarkable, that Anthony was displaying a level of understanding and knowledge that was not at all in keeping with his age. I was also aware of the general discomfort and unease that this was causing. We simply did not know how to respond. We understood almost nothing of what he was saying. He, on the other hand, was so engrossed in his subject, and so caught up in the telling, that he left no room at all for the participation of others even had we been able to follow his thinking. We were left to smile politely while uttering such meaningless comments as, 'How interesting. Is that so . . . ? How fascinating'.

We were all relieved when the time came for Anthony and his father to go. How, we wondered, was he regarded by those of his own age group?

Fiona was 16. She had joined a group of 'scholarship' students preparing for the Oxford and Cambridge examinations through a series of fortnightly seminars led by university lecturers. Fiona had achieved 'A' grades in no less than 12 O level examinations. (She subsequently gained five grade 'A's in her A levels.) She played the cello for a county orchestra, had a lovely singing voice, and was a talented sportswoman into the bargain. During the seminar discussions it had become obvious to the other students that this girl's depth and breadth of knowledge was of a different order altogether from their own. She was clearly exceptional, even among the very ablest students. 'But,' said one member of the group, 'the really surprising thing about Fiona is that she is so nice!'

During my time working as an educational psychologist with a project for developing the curriculum for very able pupils I had the opportunity to talk at length to dozens of children who had unusual talents and abilities, and their parents. These three examples, and the stories told to me by the many other children I have met over the years, epitomise the fundamental dilemmas presented by unusual devel- opment, dilemmas which need to be understood if they are ever to be resolved. They demonstrate in the simplest terms that the whole question of giftedness is one, not so much of definition, identification, categorisation and prescription, but a question of relationships in- volving the responses of persons one to another, the communication and expression of feelings, the inclusion or exclusion of individuals and groups. The main contributor to the confusion and ill-judged position-taking regarding children of exceptional ability has been the failure to recognise that at the heart of the matter we are dealing not so much with a special endowment *inside* a person, but with what happens in the dynamic relationships and communications between people.

What precisely does this mean? The explanation can perhaps best be given by looking again at the encounters with the three young people described. What was significant about the first two children's behaviour was not the behaviour as such but the reactions it provoked in those around them. The fact that little Katie, by the age of three, had developed language more consistent with that of a nine-year-old, and a social poise that appeared quite out of keeping with her age, could not be judged a problem in itself. We are all aware that children grow, develop and acquire their living skills at greatly varying rates. Children are not expected to be at similar stages in their development at particular ages. We do, however, construct certain 'limits of expectation', mental yardsticks by which we measure each new encounter. We develop an understanding of that which we judge to be a reasonable, expected, 'normal' range of behaviours. These mental yardsticks are arrived at through both our personal and our shared experiences.

It goes almost without saying that the yardsticks of 'normality' will be relative to the time, the place and the experience of those who share them. What is felt to be normal in one situation may not be so in another. Take, for example, the question of height. A person may be judged to be extremely tall in one setting yet quite normal in another. A pygmy may be a giant amongst his own tribe, yet taken for a midget in a group of Masai warriors. There are no absolutes in the questions of tallness or shortness. Extremes can only be judged in relation to the environment in which they occur. This will be true of any experience. A problem only arises where the occurrence of an experience, be it physical, social, emotional or intellectual, falls outside the normal expectations of those involved. As with Katie, the problem of the precocity of her language and social poise lay not in the child, but in the response it evoked in others, and consequently and most essentially, in the messages that passed from others to her, messages of surprise, wariness and disapproval.

The case of Anthony, the nine-year-old scientist, was similar, but with additional significant elements. His conversation, too, was startling to those around because of the incongruity of his age and the level of intellectual understanding and experience he displayed. But here the mismatch was dramatically compounded. With Katie, although her language and manner jarred and evoked unkind and unhelpful responses, at least it was possible to pursue a conversation with her, to share her interests and understand her enthusiasms. But Anthony was caught up in a world of thinking and pursuits beyond the comprehension of those around him. We were left on the sidelines of his thinking and conversation, reduced to behaving as spectators, applauding politely at appropriate moments. Again, the problem could not be said to be Anthony's brilliance in itself. Given a different setting, given a different audience there would have been no problem. The problem lay in the mismatch between his understanding and that of the people around the table. We felt inadequate, but more importantly, Anthony himself probably felt alien, and no doubt frustrated by the lack of an adequate response from his listeners.

Fiona, on the other hand, demonstrates that brilliance *per se* is not necessarily a problem. No-one denied that her talents were many and varied, that the level she achieved in the many fields of her interests were levels to which few of us can aspire. She was indeed richly and generously endowed. Yet the surprise for Fiona's companions was that *despite* her exceptional talents she was a pleasant person to have around. They not only admired, and perhaps even envied her, they liked her. How had this come about? Why should her companions be surprised by her niceness? Why should they have expected her to be otherwise? What unhappy correlates have gathered themselves alongside the notion of exceptionality, and why should such expectations have developed?

This would seem to be the heart of the matter, and the focus of concern for children and parents alike. The real question is not, 'Is this a gifted or exceptional child?' or 'Do this child's abilities qualify her to belong to a particular category which I can accept is gifted?' It is rather, 'How can I understand what is going on between this child and me, between this child and others, and between this child and her world?' It should also be, 'How can I, as the more experienced adult, enhance and guide this young person's life in order that she may make the very best of all her talents and qualities, whatever these may be?'

Chapter 2

Infancy: issues for parents

Early communication

During the past 30 years there have been dramatic advances in our understanding of infant development, and in the study of early communication between infants and those who care for them. This has been partly due to the advent of video-recording, allowing the behaviour of adults and babies to be captured on film and then analysed frame by frame. The research findings show the extraordinary sensitivity and sophistication of the responses between infants and adults from the earliest days (Wood 1988). Far from being relatively passive, indifferent to his environment, the very young baby is seen to initiate and engage in the subtlest forms of contact with his caretakers, synchronising his movements, demonstrating from birth an 'intention' to explore and respond to the aspects of his environment. Of course, in the early weeks the intentions are barely recognisable as such. Purpose and control need the maturing experience of time and practice to develop into competence. However, it is now clear that babies rapidly develop the ability to distinguish between sounds and sights and to respond selectively to them. Within weeks a baby can tell the difference between his mother's face and voice and that of others, and shows distress or pleasure according to the expression on her face or the tone of her voice. Whereas in times past we believed it did not matter too much who handled the baby, or how he was looked at or spoken to so long as it was with reasonable care, we now understand that it does, that the baby *is* aware and that the baby minds. However, despite 'knowing', 'feeling' and 'minding', the baby is in a relatively helpless position when it comes to communicating these feelings. He is dependent on the adult's ability to recognise and *interpret* any communications expressed through the cry, the gaze, the smile, and the movements of arms and hands (Wood 1988).

The infant also begins to become aware of himself and his separateness from others through the response to his actions. Dr Anthony Storr, in his book *The School of Genius*, talks about the notion of 'self' growing out of the early interactions between the baby and the mother or mother substitute, and that it is the extension and expansion of contacts with others throughout their lives that provides people with a sense of self, and an inner coherence. He quotes the psychiatrist Heinz Kohut on the importance of the relationships between the baby and the parent-figures at this early stage. Kohut said that adults need to reinforce the child's sense of self through recognising and mirroring the child's developing identity *as it actually is*, empathising with the child's feelings, responding to the child's demands with '*non-hostile firmness and non-seductive affection*'. In other words, being firm without being rejecting and not becoming a slave to the baby's demands. Kohut believed that great damage is done to children's later development where parents are unable to provide this '*empathic understanding*'. As Storr explains, developing this sense of self is like looking in a mirror: a clear and polished mirror repeatedly reflects the developing person as he actually is, thus giving him a firm and true sense of his own identity; a cracked, dirty, smeared mirror provides the child with an inaccurate and distorted picture of himself (Storr 1988).

These insights and perceptions into the behaviour of infants and the growth of personality have a particular significance for the study of exceptional children's development. We may still be unsure as to the relative importance of genetic inheritance and physical and social environment in making us who we are and in bringing about the differences between us, but even so, we can assume that we are born with differing 'response patterns'. Any mother, or any person who has closely observed newborn infants, knows that this is so. We need, in fact, claim no more than this: to be born with different response patterns inevitably sets off a train of response relationships that ensures unique development.

One could speculate that children who later develop their abilities to exceptional levels are born with a highly sensitised capacity to respond to their environment. Learning is all about experiencing. It is through our contact with our world that we grow to know our world and to develop our capacity to 'think' about it and to organise ourselves within it. If a child is born with highly sensitive response mechanisms he is likely to experience more and be more aware of his environment than an infant with slower or more muted receptivity. Whether or not there is a genetic component to the way babies respond to early experiences may be of great interest to those concerned with the academic study of human psychology. It is of much less importance to those whose business is *living* with children. What is important for them is to be able to understand what the consequences of such a possibility might be. It could mean for instance, that a highly responsive child would be acutely affected by everything that happened around him and would perceive events more intensely: sounds, images and physical sensations might be felt more strongly and thereby evoke sharper reactions.

Protecting the early relationship

Taking on responsibility for a new baby is one of the greatest challenges of all. It is a privilege and a joy, but it can also be an axious time because we know that the first two years of a baby's life set the foundations for his future growth. An adequate level of physical care is essential for the healthy development of the child's body and mind but the *quality* of parenting will have a significant impact on the child's personality and psychological well-being. We know that babies who are socially neglected or who receive too little stimulation become listless and apathetic. Babies who are actively encouraged to explore their new world tend to develop more active and inquisitive minds. Babies are also very sensitive to the emotional atmosphere. Although they may not be able to explain their feelings, they do respond to the feelings of those around them. If the baby's behaviour irritates the parent, he will sense it and some important 'messages' will begin to be communicated – messages of anger and despair, of helplessness, of wishing to escape from his presence and the burden of his care. Subconsciously the baby will begin to recognise and absorb these feelings and this may set a pattern for his relationships which will affect his emotional development. There is even some evidence arising out of recent research into post-natal depression that difficulties in the early stages of parent–child relationships can have long-term repercussions on the family. It would appear that even very young babies can detect when adults are depressed, irritable or feel very low, and they too then become less sociable and withdrawn. So it makes sense to avoid wherever possible the sources of stress that are harmful to the early relationships, and do whatever we can to create an environment which provides the security and welcome in which the baby's personality can flourish.

   In the first two years of a young child's life the prime concern for the family is to adjust to the new living arrangements and to develop satisfactory and rewarding relationships. Adjusting to a new lifestyle is never easy but for the great majority of families this is an exciting and enriching period of their lives. For some, however, the situation is less happy. When the new baby places demands on parents which are greater than they had expected they can become confused and distressed. They need extra help and support, and have to think more carefully how to safeguard the quality of the baby's developing relationships. In the early days the dynamics that are most likely to affect the adults' relationships with a baby are those which place the greatest demand on their patience and well-being: crying, sleep disturbance, and the drive to explore.

Crying

For Thomas's mother the first twelve months with her eldest son were very stressful:

> He screamed from the moment he was born. He would cry all day long, and often into the night. Nothing I did seemed to calm him or put things right. I tried leaving him alone, carrying him about, feeding him, playing with him, walking him. Nothing worked. The odd times when he slept – and he didn't sleep much either – were heaven. I dreaded his waking up. I was sure the neighbours thought it was all my fault, that I was a bad mother. I ended up almost hating the child. I often thought I might go mad and harm him. I certainly wished I'd never had him. It seemed like a nightmare. I felt I had been conned. I never imagined motherhood would be like that.

Those who have never known a really 'difficult' baby in this sense can have little idea how stressful this situation can be. Those who have will readily be able to identify with this mother's feelings. A baby's cry has a particular effect on adults; it provokes an immediate reaction. A baby's crying cannot be ignored and, if prolonged, it becomes unbearable. Crying is a survival mechanism, it is the baby's way of attracting attention. When the system works smoothly, all is well. The baby calls, the adult responds, and the baby's needs are answered. Sometimes, however, the system breaks down. The baby cries and the adult responds, but in spite of all attempts to solve the possible problem, the child does not quieten. The situation then becomes acutely uncomfortable. The baby is clearly distressed and indicates this in the only way he knows how. The adult wants to help the baby and remove any source of distress, but because the sound is so powerful an irritant there is a strong need to stop the crying itself. If all attempts to calm the baby fail, the adult can become increasingly depressed or irritated, overwhelmed by feelings of helplessness and despair. Sometimes the misery of the situation results in actual physical violence. In any event, the feelings that are aroused and transmitted between adult and child will be intense and unhappy.

There is no easy answer to the problem of a child who refuses to be soothed, but once one has attended to all the obvious possibilities of hunger, pain or other general discomforts, it is worth looking to other possible sources of distress such as over-stimulation, boredom, or the need for more physical contact.

Babies, particularly very sensitive ones, can easily become over-stimulated or exhausted by the bombardment from the myriad sensations of sound, sight and touch. The more sensitive the child, the more keenly these experiences are felt, and the more acute the distress will be, once saturation point has been reached. If a baby cries a lot, he may be overtired, over-dazzled – overwhelmed by noise and movement. Jiggling and rocking and trying to distract his attention through waving things in front of him may make matters worse. Instead, it may be better to *reduce* the input the baby is receiving. Wrapping him up snug and tight in a shawl and sitting calmly with him in a quiet place can sometimes help. Later, when a baby is bigger and stronger, a highly responsive child may get overtired much more quickly than others, simply by the amount he takes in through exploring everything around him. You may think he is by nature just a grizzly, scratchy kind of child, who is too easily upset. Again it is worth considering this behaviour in terms of 'over-sensitivity'. By carefully observing the pattern of his day and his response to prolonged periods of stimulation you may be able to anticipate the trigger points and avoid situations which put him under undue stress.

An eager, responsive baby wants to explore his world, but while he is still tiny he is dependent on adults to create situations where this can happen, where they can bring the world to him. Long ago mothers were told that babies should be left alone for long periods during the day to learn how to entertain themselves and that this was good 'training' for later life. Fortunately we no longer believe this to be a helpful or proper way to treat young children. All that babies learn through such practices is that the world is a harsh and lonely place, and that adults cannot be depended on to come when they are needed. Babies need constant contact with others. They only learn to know and understand their world by exploring it, first through sight and sound, later by touch and action. Babies become bored with particular situations. They need change and variety in appropriate measures. Now we know how much babies absorb we need to think carefully about the kind, the quality and the variety of interesting things we offer them for their entertainment.

From the very outset babies need the interest and pleasure of changing sights and sounds. The world inside the house, and the world outside, is full of possibilities, so long as the baby is in a position to see, and to watch the movement of objects and listen to the variety of sounds. Obviously, a baby who has to lie on his back looking at nothing but a blank ceiling will soon be bored; but *any* situation, looked at for too long, induces boredom. It is the *change* that maintains interest. This is what makes mobiles so fascinating. Mobiles are easy to make, fun to watch, and can be frequently varied. When buying or making mobiles you need to think about not only colour and shape but also sound and movements through the use of material such as silver foil, glossy paper, tinsel, coloured balls, bells and metal objects, in fact anything that will catch the light and breeze and capture the baby's attention. Other ideas for bringing interest to the baby's room include moving the cot about the room to vary the view; sticking pictures or different coloured shapes and patterns on the wall – or even the ceiling – and changing these from time to time; hanging wind chimes or any other light object in the window to produce changes in movement and sound. There are lots of toys designed to be attached to a baby's crib or pram, which bring interest and colour for him to see, and later encourage touch and play with his hands.

But human beings are, above all, social creatures and the source of greatest interest will be people. Parents and brothers and sisters, family and friends can all bring things of interest for the baby to see, create sounds for him to hear, introduce him to different tactile sensations. Holding, rocking, stroking, playing with fingers and toes, tickling, kissing and caressing are all forms of communication and tell the baby that he is loved and cared for, and that people are nice to be with.

Babies need lots of physical contact. They pass traumatically at birth

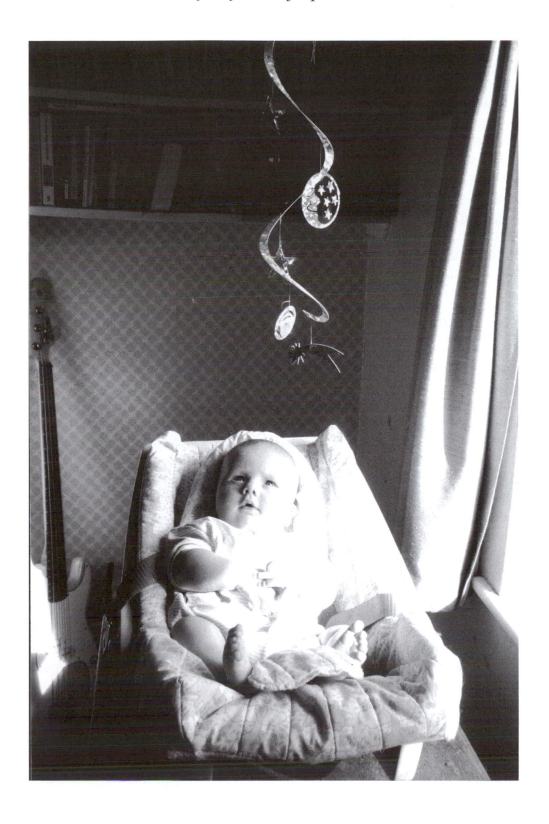

from a situation of intense 'one-ness', wrapped tight and warm inside a safe mother, to a world of space and new and puzzling sensations. The adjustment from the inside to the outside world is not easy. A highly sensitised child may suffer more than most, and feel the contrasts dramatically. Learning that you are still connected to others, despite being separate, is one of the most vital and fundamental human experiences. Babies need continued reassurance. This is seen in the way they nestle into their mother's arms and are soothed by stroking. It is a reassurance we seek throughout our lives through cuddling, hugging, and clasping hands. Some babies need more reassurance than others, particularly those that feel overwhelmed by their experiences. It is better at this stage to provide babies with lots of attention and contact rather than to suffer the consequences at a later date.

Sleep disturbance

One of the widely held beliefs about exceptionally able people is that, as small children, they needed very little sleep. Indeed, the belief has become extended so far as to suggest that extreme restlessness and poor sleeping habits are of themselves indicators of future high performance. The need for very little sleep is not, in fact, a reliable indicator at all of high intelligence or exceptional talent. Disturbed sleep patterns can have many different causes. Nevertheless, because many parents of children who show exceptional development in later years remember them as having needed very little sleep when young an association has grown up in people's minds, no doubt strengthened by the fact that where such an association occurs it was so difficult to manage. Whatever the cause, the experience of prolonged sleep disturbance is so distressing it remains engraved on the parents' memories.

   It is not hard to understand why this should be so. By the time we come as adults to look after children we have usually established our own sleep patterns according to our individual needs. Some people need much more sleep than others, others need hardly any at all. Whatever our particular pattern may be, we are likely to feel quite distressed by any alteration to our particular habits. The advent of a baby usually induces a dramatic one. How long this disturbance lasts before some kind of normalisation or compromise is established depends on the individuals involved. Anyone who has had the care of a newborn will remember the discomfort of the early weeks of having nights continually interrupted. Sleep deprivation is of course a common form of torture, so it is not surprising that parents of very young, poor-sleeping babies become acutely distressed. Fortunately for most people, babies do settle down. They gradually become able to survive longer intervals between feeds. They learn to sleep the night through. With luck, a baby will continue to need sleeping periods during the day for some time into its second year and beyond. The parent is then able to find at least some periods of relief and rest. However, not everyone is so fortunate. In the case of a 'non-sleeper' it becomes essential to find ways of surviving the discomfort of the mismatch between sleeping needs.

Several things are worth bearing in mind. First, it is important to recognise that learning to live with others does require an element of compromise, a willingness to adapt and to accept different life patterns. The learning process is not always easy, and is often uncomfortable. Personal needs may have to be modified. Progress towards harmony can be achieved only by negotiation, and negotiation implies give *and* take, not only take. Babies are setting out on the journey of life. The process of 'negotiation' is only just beginning and adults have a responsibility for sensibly and sensitively guiding the child along the way. Initially, during the stages when the baby is all 'need', dominated by the dictates of its internal mechanisms, adults must be prepared to make all the personal adjustments. But establishing the 'rights' and 'needs' of others beyond the self can still begin, even at this early stage. For a baby who goes to sleep late, bedtime can be gradually brought forward each night by a few minutes at a time, almost without the child becoming aware of it. Over a matter of weeks a reasonable and acceptable target can be reached and then kept to. Similarly, babies who wake very early can gradually become accustomed to waiting awhile before adults come to attend to them. Children cannot be forced to go to sleep or prevented from waking early, but they can learn that human entertainment has its 'closing' and its 'starting' times.

It is most important to work towards establishing firm but reasonable routines. If not, the adults lose sight of their own rights and those of their partners and other members of the family. Exhausted parents have little energy or patience to deal with the daytime demands of active infants. All eventually suffer. If a baby goes to sleep late or wakes early, he can be given toys, books, and music to entertain him during the time that others are normally asleep. It will also be worth thinking about other sources of help, especially during the early months. Where there are two parents, then the responsibility can and should be shared. Mothers or principal caretakers have just as much need of sleep in order to face the demands of a day caring for children as do their partners, whatever the demands of their day. If there is only one parent, then some other help and relief should be sought. The help of relatives, friends and neighbours can be invaluable, if only to give time for a midday rest and a chance to restore some physical and mental energy. As with crying, the important thing to keep in mind is that, by safeguarding their own health and well-being, parents are also protecting their relationship with the child, and making sure he grows up in a welcoming and contented environment.

Play and exploration

In order to learn about his world the baby must explore it. While still a helpless infant he will explore his surroundings with his eyes. Later, as control over movement develops and coordination becomes increasingly refined, the exploration will be extended through all the other senses: touching, banging, squeezing, shaking, tasting. By such means the child learns to 'know' his world and to learn the properties of the objects within it. Play is a way of further exploring and then testing what is being learnt. Exploration and play are essential ingredients of both physical and intellectual growth.

As adults we love to watch babies becoming more skilful. We watch eagerly for each new sign of progress. We identify with the child's pleasure in each new experience and share his excitement and surprise as new things are discovered. This sharing of experience between adult and child is perhaps the most crucial and significant element in early human experience and one that will lay the foundations for all future relationships. Without a caring and participating adult, the child will undoubtedly still explore his world because human beings have an innate drive to explore and to 'know' our environments. But, as was

mentioned earlier, it is in the mirror of the adult's face that the child learns to interpret the new-found knowledge and to attach significance to it. In his book on the development of children's thinking Professor David Wood describes the complex interplay between mothers and their infants, where through eye contact and eye pointing they direct their baby's attention to objects and experiences in the environment, and then by describing and commenting on what is being observed, they provide a language and a meaning for the child's experience (Wood 1988).

The child reacts to each new skill he masters, not only in terms of the immediate effect it has on him, but also the effect it produces in others. Pleasure expressed by the adult evokes pleasure and satisfaction in the child. The two share the delight of a new discovery, of a new skill developing. The growth of understanding and skills becomes associated with the joy of love between human beings. Where this growth of skill and knowledge through exploration is not matched or mirrored by a 'human response', it remains as mere knowledge: objective, practical, impersonal. It may be that it is in the quality of these shared experiences, from the earliest moments of life, that future attitudes to learning and relationships are determined.

Play and exploration are instinctive and universal needs. However, in some children the drive to explore is so urgent and so excessive that their families are overwhelmed. Eager, restless, inquisitive babies, ones whose very energy may result in their absorbing their world at such a rate that they become 'exceptional', can cause serious problems for their caretakers. In the early months such a child can become intensely frustrated by the distance between the need to explore and his ability to satisfy this desire. Such children see or know what they want to do, but cannot physically manage to achieve it, or, if they do, cause chaos and destruction in the doing. We all know of children who are into everything. No sooner is the back turned than televisions, videos and electronic gadgets are turned on, objects pulled from every drawer and cupboard, unexpected and disastrous uses found for precious possessions. Oliver was one such child. From tiny, his main interest in any toy or object was to take it apart, if necessary with a hammer. Everything he touched was reduced to bits, to his mother's despair and even anger. As he grew older and the destruction extended remorselessly throughout the house, their relationship became increasingly stressed.

It is very hard indeed to remain calm in the face of such unrelenting enthusiasm and energy – very difficult to share the pleasure of the

child's new-found skill. It is also extremely tiring. Ingenuity and a sense of humour are essential. Adults need to recognise and accept that a child's desire to explore is instinctive and natural, and that he will not be able to respond to 'reason'. Continuing to explore, despite his parents' displeasure, is not being 'naughty'. Naughtiness is deliberate disobedience – an intention to disregard an instruction or to do deliberate damage. Babies cannot 'intend' in this way: their thinking is too primitive. A baby's need to explore his world must be satisfied if deep frustration and later depression are to be avoided. The more eager, restless and inquisitive the child, the more potential there is for such frustration, and the greater the need there will be for careful organisation and planning. During the period of intense activity, at a time when the child's coordination is still at a primitive level, it makes sense to arrange your house and possessions so that potential danger and distress will be avoided.

Play offers the adult and child a precious opportunity to set the foundations for learning on human grounds. It is vital that this foundation is a loving one. If, through the exercising of his natural desires, the child encounters disapproval and anger, he will become confused. Curiosity and a zest for life will become associated with adult disapproval and anger. The consequences for future learning and future relationships are obvious. If, on the other hand, the child's discoveries are complemented by the adult's pleasure, then discovery becomes a human joy, a means of experiencing 'shared adventures'.

Chapter 3

The preschool years

Early development of self-concept

The period of near-complete dependency, from the moment of birth to the time when the child becomes physically and emotionally able to explore beyond the environment of the home, is the foundation stage for healthy future development. This crucial period is normally safeguarded by the synchronisation of physical and intellectual and emotional growth. As physical strength and coordination increase, so too do the opportunities for exploration and therefore for learning. New experiences bring new awareness both of the physical world and of relationships with other human beings.

This moving out into the world brings with it exciting new opportunities for growth, but also increased possibilities of stress, particularly for children whose development is in any way unusual. This may certainly be the case for children whose physical and intellectual development are markedly out of phase. Where, for instance, physical development has proceeded normally, but where intellectual development is delayed. Or where intellectual development or physical development is exceptionally precocious.

The learning about ourselves begins from the moment of birth. Babies, as we have seen, begin to learn about the *world* through the joint experiencing of their actions and the effect these have on others. They learn about *themselves* as a result of interactions with others. Throughout our lives we continue to learn about ourselves from the encounters we have with others. It is in the mirrors of these encounters that we come to think of ourselves as clever or stupid, good or bad, kind or cruel. One unfortunate result of this process of learning is that some children can grow up thinking ill of themselves through a history of unhappy encounters.

By living and growing together people also develop a shared understanding of what is 'normal'. As far as children's development is concerned, certain stages of growth, certain skills are expected to emerge and develop within given age ranges. Thus, in our western society, we expect that babies will begin to babble and practise sound patterns during the first year, that words will become intelligible from 9 months onwards, and that words will be put together in simple sentences between 18 months and 2½ years. We also expect babies to begin to sit up before their first birthday, to crawl any time between 9 and 15 months, and to walk by the time they are 18 months. These are called the 'milestones' of early development and are watched for with interest by all concerned. Similar progress is expected in the child's ability to use his hands in manipulating objects and in his understanding of the relationships between them.

Awareness of these shared understandings becomes apparent when a child's development does not match our expectations. This is as true when the development is unusually slow as it is when it appears precocious. An infant who learns to put reasonable and intelligible sentences together before the age of 12 months is unusual. So is the child who, with no formal teaching, learns to read by the age of two. We do not understand why or how such skills have developed so early, but their appearance at this age will certainly surprise. The problem lies, not in the precocity itself, but in the effect it has on the audience, and the messages that will thereafter be conveyed to the child from all whom he meets. The messages convey a feeling that he is different, unusual, remarkable and, in some cases, not entirely welcome. The child will certainly feel bewildered. He has no ability to reflect on his behaviour, and will register only the feelings that his presence and unselfconscious actions provoke in others. Even worse, these feelings may be highly ambivalent, a mixture of pleasure and pride in the early achievements, and apprehension or even rejection because of the surprise they cause. Even from the earliest age, mixed messages, ambivalent feelings, unpredictable responses, cause greater distress to small children than any straightforward expressions of anger.

What are the implications for such a child, when their experience of people and activities widens beyond the immediate family? How might others respond? After all, it *is* surprising to meet a child of two who speaks like a five-year-old, or who can read fluently. It does take one aback to see a four-year-old writing complex adventure stories or demonstrating advanced mathematical understanding. It can be difficult not to express amazement at the obvious skills of infant artists or musicians. The danger is that from such reactions the child can learn to think of herself as an 'extraordinary' person, someone special, someone who is superior to others. Believing that one is abnormal (in whatever sense) is a powerful isolator.

Unfortunately, highly intelligent or talented children not only excite comment but may also be encouraged to perform in front of others, like circus creatures, to demonstrate their skills and receive applause. In such circumstances a child may develop attitudes and behaviour which isolate and alienate her. This was clearly the case with the little girl Katie, described earlier. A vicious circle is set in motion. It is not a question of denying the talents of a child or pretending that she does not possess the skills she so patently does. It is rather a question of encompassing the skills within the framework of the child's 'normality'. If people are aware of the power of the messages being conveyed to children at this stage then much greater care can be given to the way unusual development is met. Parents of children with unusual talents or abilities must do what they can to forestall the surprised reactions of others. They can forewarn relatives and friends. They can see that nothing is said to the child that will suggest to him that he is 'abnormal'. A child should never be put 'on show'. Any particular talents children possess should be accepted and enjoyed alongside all the other aspects of behaviour, no more, no less. They must be allowed to develop a sense of belonging and of being 'as others', as well as enjoying the feeling of being unique, and special. No child should feel that her need to be loved and valued is won through the display of talents. An American writer with much experience of exceptional children observed:

> The most important thing the world can give to the gifted child is a welcome and an acknowledgement of their human as well as their intellectual capacities. While this is a need all children share, the gifted child's own accomplishments, by being outstanding, may work to his own detriment, if they alone are the means by which his world acknowledges him. (Vail 1979)

Relating to other children

It may be much more difficult to help the exceptional child to form relationships with other children. While she is still very small, contacts with other young children depend very much on the sociability of the parents and how often they meet together with other adults and their children. Very young children tend to play *alongside*, rather than *with* each other. Nevertheless, from very early on we can see the beginnings of shared play, with the taking and offering of play-objects between one another. Even at this early play stage, it is also noticeable that the behaviour of some children affects that of others. Personal styles are already quite well marked. Some young children are energetic and forceful, others are more cautious. Dominant and sturdy-minded children with a boisterous style of approach can be seen to shock and distress their more timid companions. They seem literally to launch themselves upon the newcomer: hair is pulled, eyes are poked at, toys are snatched away. Great excitement and pleasure is usually shown by the aggressor during these encounters; less by the victim. When children are very young, the situations are usually resolved by adults: children are separated, consoled, reprimanded, toys are restored to rightful owners and new diversions found.

As the child grows older contacts with other children become more frequent, and more 'play' takes place between the children themselves. They spend longer together and evolve more of the activities themselves. The bright child and her parents may welcome the additional source of exploration and interest such experiences provide. They may be eager to make use of other resources such as toddler groups, playgroups or nursery classes. A wider network of social contacts and the opportunities for exploration and new learning may be just what is needed to satisfy the bright child's eager curiosity. For most children this is so, and the new stage in the family's situation is a happy and rewarding one. For a few, it can also be rather more problematical. Many parents recount how difficult it was to integrate their child into the play of other toddlers. Play is a complex activity, with its own developmental stages and styles. Children can play on their own. They can also play with others. Where play is a shared activity it depends for success on some common agreements and shared understandings between those involved. At the simplest, most primitive level, it calls upon skills of cooperation, adaptability, compromise, the 'give-and-take' transactions.

The problem for very bright or precocious children is that they are often, intellectually at least, several steps ahead of their peers in terms of their play interests; they are often operating at a more sophisticated level.

One often sees such children start playing with another child or with a group of children, but becoming quickly impatient with the activities. They want to take over the leadership, alter the game sequence, redefine the rules. Emotionally they may be no more mature than their companions, so when they are frustrated they may throw tantrums or try to wreck other children's activities. The result is miserable for everyone concerned. The bright child may be enormously disappointed. She wants to play with others but the play on offer bores or frustrates her. She believes that the others are 'stupid', and cannot understand why *they* do not understand. In turn, the other children are likely to resent the destruction of the rhythm of their own play. No-one likes being made to feel stupid. As a result they avoid contact with the discomfort-making child and they may reject her from the group.

What often happens next is the precocious child tries to join a group of older children. However, this is not always successful. Older children often resent the intrusion. They will either use the child as a butt for their own play, or find it amusing to encourage behaviour which gets the child into trouble. Either way the precocious child is not included in a friendship group and may continue to disrupt the activities of others, or retreat to the safer world of home. There she can defend herself from the misery of rejection by dismissing others as not being worth the trouble, and concentrating on activities which will bring the comfort of adult approval. Such children experience a distressing split in their lives: wanting to play and join with others, finding it frustrating and confusing when they do so. They are unable to find a satisfactory way round the relationship problem so they often turn to knowledge to fill the gap. They discover that they can restrict their explorations to intellectual discoveries. They learn to depend on adults for approval, and to gain this through intellectual prowess. Considerable tact and creative thinking by adults is needed to handle such situations. It may be a question of trying to achieve some kind of compromise. Parents may need to be actively, though tactfully, involved in helping the child with her relationships, looking for occasions where the child can take part comfortably in a group of others of a similar age, as well as opportunities for her to develop interests at her own intellectual level. They will need to help create situations in which the taking part does not depend on everyone having the same level of ability.

There are lots of opportunities for children to find ways of enjoying doing things together within the home itself and in the immediate surroundings of most neighbourhoods: helping with the cooking and shopping, through painting and modelling; games of make-believe, through physical activities and visits to places of local interest – the list is endless. Where a child has difficulty in managing her contact with others on her own, adults can ease the way by first inviting just one child to share a supervised activity or 'treat' outing, and then as relationships develop either by extending the time of contact or the range of activities. More children can be added to form a larger group. So long as the precocious child has contact with others of a similar age and some experience of taking part with them on some mutually rewarding activity, then the foundations for constructive relationships will be maintained. It is also important for the child to be able to share interests and experiences at her own intellectual level. Here it may be necessary to look for others with similar interests, even older children or adults, and to bring them together from time to time. The National Association for Gifted Children (NAGC) and the association for Children of High Intelligence (CHI) provide a service for children and their families.

There is no doubt that some children present real challenges to the skills, energy and patience of those who care for them. Adults need to call upon their own ingenuity and also on the experience of others. There are many useful books and other resources on the market which help parents play an active role in their children's early learning (see

Play as a shared activity

reference section). In particular, Joan Beck's *How to Raise a Brighter Child,* and Joan Freeman's *Bright as a Button* provide a wealth of ideas for encouraging language, perception, early number concepts, interests in scientific investigations, and creative thinking. Many of the suggestions are creative, practical and relatively simple to organise. They both emphasise the need for children to work towards their own solutions and create their own unique experiences (Beck 1968, Freeman 1991).

Family relationships

Although we have been mainly considering the issues involved with the widening of the exceptional child's experience beyond the family and the home, we need to look at implications for the family itself. An unusually bright or talented child is likely to absorb a disproportionate share of the family's attention. When precocious development occurs, the family may need to take a serious look at the way the family interest is being shared. If it becomes unbalanced with one member receiving the lion's share, there may be unhelpful consequences with the precocious child developing an unrealistic sense of her own importance. This may result in her devaluing the rights of other siblings and to think disparagingly of others. She herself risks becoming an object of envy and dislike. Brothers and sisters who feel neglected may come to feel jealous and rejecting of the child they see as taking all their parents' attention. There is some evidence that where the focus of parental interest is centred on one child whom they identify as exceptional, the talents of the other siblings are undervalued. The family is the first community the child meets and one of the central functions of the family at this stage is to help children discover how important other people are. So, it is essential that the early experience within the family helps a child to learn to respect others, to cooperate, to wait one's turn, sometimes to modify one's own demands for the sake of a common need. Parents who do not provide such teaching provide a disservice to their children, as they will find great difficulty in establishing happy relationships in groups outside the home.

A conflict in management within the family may also occur during the so-called traumatic period around the three-year-old time. This is often a difficult stage for all parents to manage. Children are becoming aware of their growing competence and independence and begin to challenge their parents' authority. It is the stage of the dramatic 'Nos' and the temper tantrums. The child, caught up in the fierceness of her desires and her frustration at being prevented from immediately gratifying them, is often overwhelmed by the strength of her feelings. She may fear that the sheer intensity of her anger will destroy the object of her rage. What the child needs above all is to find that the world is safe and that it can withstand her onslaughts, that her parents remain in command and therefore the safe protectors they were previously known to be. Parents must be able to reassure the child that no matter how angry or how bad the feelings are, they can be managed and contained. Once the boundaries have been tested and found to hold, the child is then safe to continue to explore.

One of the major problems for intellectually precocious children is that they may feel insecure during this period. They gain glimpses of their parents' frailty at a time when emotionally they cannot cope with anything less than parental infallibility. A number of adolescents who remember this period describe consciously 'outwitting' their parents, of feeling scornful of their parents' confusion and distress. The youngsters talk of the shock of discovering the ability to manipulate adults. Their world felt fundamentally insecure. If one has the care of such a child, it is most important to remember at all times, however clever and intellectually logical the child's arguments might be, that young children need to find that the parents *are* in control and will protect them from themselves. It is important for parents to be clear in their minds as to what they feel is right, what should happen, when and how, and to follow their decisions through, calmly but firmly. Good parenting for all children requires sensitive but firm management. Very bright and able children are no exception.

This chapter has concentrated on the difficulties that may arise when a young child's development is precocious. While there may be problems and uncertainties this can be a wonderful stage in a parent's relationship with a child. It offers the adult the opportunity and privilege of returning to rediscover the wonder of one's surroundings, to look again at things previously taken for granted and to share in real excitement with the innocent delight of a child. The secret of sustaining the pleasure lies in the willingness to join the children at their level, to understand their need to explore, to provide a wide range of suitable learning opportunities and to respond sensitively to the inevitable frustrations when they find they cannot do everything they want.

Chapter 4

Starting school

Establishing the partnership

It takes a whole village to raise a child.

(Akan Proverb)

David and Sarah were nearly five when I first met them. David was about to start school and his parents were worried about the way his new teachers would respond to his difficult behaviour. Sarah had already been admitted early to her infant school at her parents' request as she was understood to be exceptionally bright. David's parents and Sarah's head teacher had both contacted me for advice. Here were two different problems presented from two different perspectives, but together they illustrate some of the most commonly encountered sources of difficulty at this important stage in children's development.

David had been a difficult child from the start. As a baby he was very restless. He walked early, explored relentlessly and had kept his parents constantly on their toes. He had shown little sense of danger, climbing all over the furniture, jumping from alarming heights, experimenting with whatever came to hand. By the age of two he was already showing an interest in reading. He had started to recognise signs, and soon began identifying articles by their labels both in the home and in shops. He seemed to 'understand' the process without being taught. When David was offered a place at the local playgroup his parents were delighted. They welcomed the chance of a break from the constant supervision, and felt he would enjoy the additional stimulation of group activities. Their pleasure was short-lived.

David's exuberant behaviour was not appreciated by the children or by the playgroup supervisors. Complaints escalated. Soon David's mother began to dread the moment she went to collect him each morning. Almost inevitably some incident would be mentioned to her. She was aware that the word was being spread among the mothers of other children in the group and that she was being criticised for her failure to control her child. His behaviour was affecting the way she was being judged as a person. She was also aware of a feeling of disapproval from playgroup staff that David could read. She sensed they thought she was pressuring the child to satisfy her own ambitions. Her explanations had been listened to politely but with scepticism. She was warned that both David's unruly behaviour and his precocity would be bound to cause difficulties at his new school. In short, David's parents were encouraged to feel thoroughly anxious, especially about the prospect of his starting school.

Sarah's parents, on the other hand, had requested an early admission to school. They had told the head teacher that she was exceptionally bright, was already reading fluently and able to write independently. They felt she needed the structure of school to satisfy her intellectual curiosity. The head teacher was a little reluctant, but finally agreed to admit Sarah when she was only four and a half. A week after she started school, Sarah's parents returned to talk to the teachers. The child, they said, was unhappy. She was apparently disappointed with what was being offered and frustrated by the lack of 'real' work. She was bored

'David's exuberant behaviour was not appreciated . . .'

by spending so much time in play activities. She wanted to write and do sums, and did not like having to play with sand and water. Sarah's parents wanted to know what the teacher was doing in the way of formal teaching, and asked to see the children's workbooks. Not unnaturally the teacher felt threatened by such a questioning approach. Defensive attitudes were struck by both sides.

The start of formal schooling is a particularly sensitive time for parents. Of course many will have used child-care services, or their child may have attended a playgroup or a nursery school. For them, the start of formal schooling will be easier as the process of separation and the sharing of the responsibility of care is more gradual. Nevertheless, the start of *formal* schooling is a milestone. It signals explicitly and emphatically that the responsibility for the care and upbringing of a child is a community venture: a responsibility in which parents have the major role, but one where others make an increasingly important contribution. Some parents may find this hard to accept and a source of anxiety. This is especially likely if their child's development is in any way unusual.

Sharing the care of their child also presents parents with a new perspective on their own identity. They are faced, perhaps for the first time in their lives, with the unavoidable fact that their good name depends not only on how *they* behave or on the relationships that they themselves are able to establish, but on the behaviour and social skills of another person. They are judged by the way their child behaves. Their reputation both as parents and as persons in their own right becomes dependent on their child. This is an alarming realisation for most people. Small wonder so much effort goes into ensuring that children conform to socially accepted forms of behaviour!

Parents may also find themselves, again perhaps for the first time, in a situation where they realise that they are not the only experts as far as their child is concerned. As the circle widens, and other people begin to work with the child, new knowledge and understandings about his personality, capabilities and needs begin to develop. The parents' perspectives become only part of the picture. Sometimes their views and opinions may be questioned, or worse, not believed. Whatever the case, parents will naturally feel apprehensive about their first encounters with school and teachers, and wonder whether their child's needs will be recognised and treated with sensitivity. Where both parties, parents and school staff, handle these early relationships with care and tact, there is usually a smooth transition to the new

Starting school is a sensitive time for parents

environment. Where people become defensive this can work against the best interests of the child. It is vital at this stage for schools and parents to work in partnership to resolve, rather than dismiss, whatever anxieties each might feel.

Partnership with parents is now very much on the agenda for all schools, particularly since the implementation of the 1994 Code of Practice for children with special educational needs. Attitudes and practice in schools have undergone significant changes in recent years, with the requirement for greater accountability and with parents encouraged to take a more active interest. Most schools have developed effective strategies for keeping in touch with parents, and providing regular and detailed information about their child's progress. However, much of the communication is still a 'one-way' affair, with the emphasis being more on information-giving, than information-sharing. Practice is often best in nursery and primary phase schools where it is easier to meet on a regular basis. It is vital that, right from the start, parents and schools develop an expectation of a partnership which will carry through to the rest of the child's education.

'A meaningful exchange of information and views . . .'

Partnership, of course, is not always easy to achieve, depending as it does on hard work, understanding and trust. It can only develop where all those concerned wish to share their experiences and are prepared to demonstrate to one another that they value the varied skills and contributions each brings to the relationship.

In the cases of David and Sarah the situation was resolved without too much difficulty, once both parents and school were able to see how much could be gained from trusting cooperation. David's new teacher invited his parents to share with her the kinds of difficulties they had faced in managing his excessive energy, and to advise her on how best to respond to his need to boss other children around. Together they agreed on a policy with regard to handling the child and to meet regularly to see that all was going well. They were able to discuss David's advanced reading skills, and consider what kind of balance should be sought between the development of other basic skills, and the need to provide all the other vital experiences of shared play and creative work.

Sarah's situation was a little more complex but also had a happy outcome. The main difficulty was the lack of appreciation between parents and teacher of each other's points of view. Once they had shared their thoughts and experiences, many areas of agreement were reached. Sarah's teacher was able to explain the philosophy behind her approach and to validate the activities that Sarah's parents had dismissed as 'play'. She was able to offer the parents a view of the child's needs in terms of relating to other children in a way they had not been able to appreciate before. The teacher admitted that she herself had never met a child with such advanced reading and writing skills at this age, and made it plain that this presented her with a real professional challenge. Sarah's parents, once they believed that their child's special abilities were recognised and taken seriously, were able to consider sympathetically the problems faced by the teacher, and conceded that Sarah's frustrations were probably due more to social upsets than lack of intellectual challenge in the class. Instead of criticising they offered to help where possible. They agreed to keep in touch about what Sarah was doing at home so that the teacher knew on what interests to build and which to reinforce. They also offered their own support for school activities.

Both David and Sarah were lucky enough to have parents and teachers who were honest enough to admit to each other their mutual need for advice. As a result, though their lives in school have not been without their moments, they have both continued to do well, remaining active and enthusiastic and becoming well accepted among their peers, despite their obvious exceptional abilities.

Balancing intellectual and social needs

A child may enter school at the age of five with skills so precocious that the teacher is unsure how best to structure his learning. If the child already reads fluently, writes clearly and with ease, or demonstrates mathematical competence way beyond his years, the infant teacher may doubt whether she has the experience or the resources to meet his needs. She may also face the dilemma of wanting to build upon existing knowledge and skills while at the same time ensuring that the experiences she provides are appropriate for the child's emotional stage of development.

Take, for instance, the case of another child, Rebecca, who started school when she was 4 years 8 months. Technically she could read at the level of a twelve-year-old. Not only could she read fluently, but she clearly understood what she read. She was able to alter the inflexion of her voice to mark changes in the events of the narrative, and to give sensible definitions for the more difficult words.

A teacher is clearly faced with a problem in a situation such as this, if only at the level of providing appropriate reading materials. Obviously careful thought has to be given to the kind of books young children read. A child must be allowed access to a full and varied reading experience, but the ideas and the information she encounters should also be suitable for her emotional growth and her ability to respond in feeling as well as in intellectual terms. Some books that the child might technically be able to read are quite unsuitable in terms of content, since they are written to meet the interests of young adolescents. Books written specifically for children of Rebecca's age were of limited interest to her and lacked the breadth and richness of vocabulary she enjoyed. However, it is not always necessary to see progress in reading as the ability to read ever more demanding texts. On the contrary it is often more appropriate for children to be encouraged to use a simple story as the basis for a range of creative activities. This might include expanding and elaborating the theme through writing or recording, researching stories which have similar events or characters, writing a play on a similar theme. The able child is often just as excited by extending, enriching and transforming material as by acquiring new knowledge. It is certainly possible even at this early stage to help children become skilful at selecting resources and reading materials to satisfy their interests and further their own learning. In situations such as Rebecca's it is essential that teacher and parent consult together and decide jointly what is the best approach.

A similar dilemma can be faced when a child starts school with precocious mathematical ability. Teachers tend to be wary of unusual mathematical skills at this stage. They may suspect that the ability to manipulate figures may not be matched by a proper conceptual understanding. They can also be anxious about their own ability to provide adequately for such children, and worried that parents may begin to question their competence. This can sometimes lead to the teacher insisting the same exercises be followed and practised by all children, even when this means a child rehearsing familiar routines. For the able mathematician this is often unnecessary and causes resentment and frustration. Again children are better served by having opportunities to be creative with their existing skills, and being encouraged to look for new ways of finding solutions, calculating answers, exploring new sequences and patterns. The same can be said for teaching and learning in science. Fortunately, with the advent of the National Curriculum as a framework for learning, teachers now have a much clearer guide for their planning and teaching. The breadth of mathematical and scientific experience required by the programmes of study provides sufficient potential challenge for most children at this early age. Nevertheless, there will be some exceptional children whose level of skill and understanding will present problems even to reasonably experienced infant school teachers and they will need to seek advice from friends and colleagues. It may also be necessary to consult with teachers of older children, or look for help from interested adults in the community who can offer time to work with the child in school. There can be no blueprint for the teaching of such children and the needs of each will be unique.

Teachers of children with precocious intellectual ability must also be mindful of the need to safeguard the balance in their learning experiences, and ensure that the children have appropriate oppor-tunities to foster their social and emotional development. Some-times parents of very able children put greater value on their need to make progress in formal aspects of their learning and undervalue the importance of play and social learning. But play is an essential part of the learning process. It allows the child to explore and experiment, to discover the dynamics of cause and effect, to build imaginary worlds, to rehearse new roles, to practise new skills. Play is the basis of early social relationships, where children learn to share and to cooperate. By the age of five children's play has become a complex and sophisticated process where they are learning not only with, but from, each other. A child who has not learnt to play is seriously at risk. If parents are worried about their children 'playing' in school this must be openly discussed so that the purpose and the value to the child are more readily appreciated.

Reducing a child's frustration

There are other problems arising from mismatch within a child's pattern of development, or between a child and his social environment, that call upon not so much the professional competence of a teacher as human sensitivity. Exceptionally intelligent children are liable to suffer terrible frustrations, particularly when they are very young and their physical coordination is as yet immature. The problem is that they so often know what it is they want to do, but lack the physical ability to achieve it. This is often most apparent in the question of writing. Learning to write is itself a laborious business. It requires care, patience and reasonable coordination. For very young children it can be a highly unsatisfactory way of expressing one's thoughts and ideas, rarely producing what was intended. The expression of the thinking is limited not so much by the quality of the ideas as by the physical difficulty of guiding the pen across the page. Unfortunately the process of writing transforms the potentially exciting communication of ideas into a struggle between the pen and paper and the child. The greater the wealth of ideas and the desire to communicate, the greater the frustration. Sensitivity is all-important in understanding how such frustration affects very intelligent and imaginative children.

Alongside formal writing instruction and practice, such children need to be offered a wide variety of opportunities for sharing their interests and plans. It is, of course, important that ideas be given physical expression, that they be recorded in ways in which children can 'own' them, and with pride. The rapid advance in the use of information and communication technology, with the access this provides to the use of graphics and illustration, has provided a whole new world of possibilities for teachers and for children, and in the future this is likely to help overcome many of the difficulties that impede children's learning today, particularly for those who find difficulty with the early stages of writing.

Frustration caused by the inability to give proper expression to ideas reveals itself in other ways. Many teachers and parents will have encountered children who, even at a very young age, work at particular projects almost to the point of obsession. They appear to be driven by some inner dream, refusing to be influenced by the reassurance of others, insisting on working and reworking until the plan has been perfected. If the dream evades them, the offending object will often be suddenly rejected or violently and angrily destroyed. This desire for perfection can be a source of intense distress to children; it can also baffle and irritate those who have to care for them. With such children there is little to be gained by praising the rejected product. If what they have produced is not right, then it is not right. We must bear in mind that such children depend as much on internal evaluation as praise from others. Parents and teachers have to find tactful ways of helping children achieve their aims, by offering advice, by helping them with part of the task, and by reassuring them and helping them cope with failures when they occur.

Starting school is a critical moment in a child's life. It sets a pattern for learning and social relationships which can affect the way children respond to school in the longer-term. It is vital that these important early experiences are managed well and that teachers and parents establish a trusting and collaborative partnership.

Chapter 5

A climate for learning

Human needs

Children spend a very large proportion of their life in school. They go there to *learn* in the widest possible interpretation of the word. They learn about themselves, about being a person within a group of others, about the community in which they live, and about the world around them. The kind of learning that occurs, and how it is acquired, will to a large extent determine the progress the children make and the understandings they develop about themselves and others. In other words it helps determine the kind of people they become.

Children learn best when they feel safe, secure and at home in their classrooms. The principal task for schools and teachers is to create environments in which *all* children grow to be confident in themselves as learners and as people. In other words, to build a 'community for learning'.

In order to develop this confidence children need to feel welcome and valued. Maslow 1954, an American psychologist, provided a most useful structure for understanding the path to self-fulfilment and the ability to become what he termed a 'self-actualised' person, who is capable of building a rich and fulfilling life and of contributing to the greater good. He proposed that, as human beings, we have a hierarchy of needs, each level of which must be satisfied to a reasonable degree before a person is capable of progressing to a higher level.

We all share the basic physical needs for food and shelter, we all need to have a reasonable measure of certainty and consistency in our environment, to love and be loved, to feel we belong and that others are interested in our welfare, to feel good about ourselves, and to develop a sense of purpose in our lives. When a particular level of need

Maslow's Hierarchy of Needs

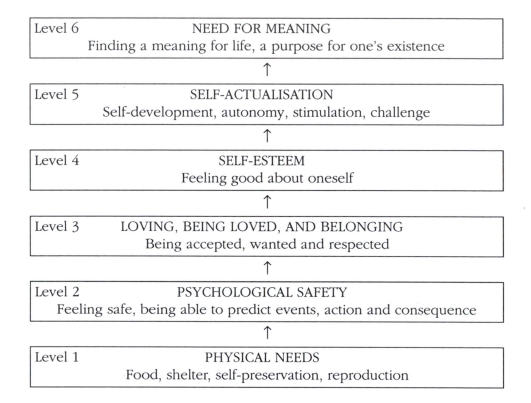

Level 6	NEED FOR MEANING
	Finding a meaning for life, a purpose for one's existence

↑

Level 5	SELF-ACTUALISATION
	Self-development, autonomy, stimulation, challenge

↑

Level 4	SELF-ESTEEM
	Feeling good about oneself

↑

Level 3	LOVING, BEING LOVED, AND BELONGING
	Being accepted, wanted and respected

↑

Level 2	PSYCHOLOGICAL SAFETY
	Feeling safe, being able to predict events, action and consequence

↑

Level 1	PHYSICAL NEEDS
	Food, shelter, self-preservation, reproduction

remains unsatisfied a person's energies become focussed on that aspect of their life.

So, for instance, if children are malnourished and ill cared for they will have little interest in anything other than finding comfort and food. If children's lives are full of distress and uncertainties and they are never sure who will be at home to look after them, they will spend much of their time seeking reassurance, and trying to establish some predictability in their lives. The level of 'loving and being loved', being a valued member of a group, is the pivotal level in the hierarchy, *the* essential human need, which must be satisfied if children are to develop a positive view of themselves. The need is so great that if love and respect do not come easily and naturally from those around, children will seek out other sources. They will find ways of gaining attention, soliciting affection, buying their way into a group. If these strategies fail to get them the interest and affection they crave many children will find alternative ways of seeking personal reassurance.

Growing up 'gifted' can be difficult, as Joan Freeman so ably describes in her book *Gifted Children Growing Up* (Freeman 1991). It can be confusing for parents to have a child whose development is unusual, where they may be unsure how best to manage their relationships or provide for their needs. It can be challenging for the teachers responsible for providing suitable learning experiences. And it can be problematic for such children when they find that their interests and abilities set them apart from others of their age. The emergence of an unusual talent or ability is a challenge to us all. It requires us to think more carefully and creatively. It forces us to recognise that we may all need help in working out satisfactory solutions to any problems we may encounter.

Children with exceptional abilities have the same fundamental needs as others. They need to be liked. They need people to respect them for who they are, more than for what they do. They need teachers to recognise their stage of development and their particular learning styles. They do best when they are given a balance of support, encouragement and challenge, and where they have opportunities to explore their learning and practise their skills in as wide a variety of settings as possible.

But exceptional ability brings with it many 'special' features which we need to remember when working out ways of living and learning together. Children with exceptional abilities can face particular difficulties in developing a sense of belonging, in having their needs recognised and in being offered learning opportunities that encourage and sustain their interest and excitement. They often grow up feeling different. Throughout their infancy and early childhood they may be made to feel 'special' through comments made about them and by responses to their behaviour. They learn to think of themselves as 'more' than others – more skilful, more talented, more deserving of time and attention. Their precocious behaviour and interests may make other children, and adults, feel uncomfortable, as Anthony did when he came to tea in my home, and this may reinforce their feeling of not belonging, of not being easy to be with. They can become 'Able Mis-fits', as Kellmer-Pringle 1970, called them in her study of very able troubled children.

Since feelings of belonging, of being loved and made welcome, and feeling good about oneself are so essential to our emotional wellbeing, 'unusual' children may resort to ways of having these needs satisfied which create further distance between themselves and others. As we have seen, if children of their own age are found to be unsatisfactory companions they may seek the company of older children, or they may court the attention of adults who will at least make them feel good about their accomplishments. If their greater understanding, skill, or work rate causes difficulties with their peers, they may consciously limit their performance and disguise their abilities. Other ways of gaining attention may include attempts to buy their way into the group, or to play the class clown. Alternatively they may decide that people are not worth the effort and that their own company and the solitary pursuit of their own interests are more rewarding. None of these strategies is satisfactory for the child's longer-term wellbeing. A child should never be allowed to feel a 'mis-fit'. There should always be a way in which each child's uniqueness can be welcomed and their contribution valued.

Fostering relationships

During the primary years of schooling children spend much of their time within the physical environment of a particular classroom, with a particular group of children, and with a particular teacher. The actual classroom or the teacher may change each year, but the class group is unlikely to do so. For those children who find themselves unacceptable to their peers, or in an unsatisfactory relationship with their teacher, life in school becomes a punishing experience.

Friends are essential at all stages of life. Without friends many of the activities we undertake are meaningless. People without friends are an exceptionally vulnerable group. Their health and welfare is constantly at risk. The ability to make and to retain friends is therefore a great gift and one which we should cherish and foster in all our children. The majority of children with exceptional abilities do establish satisfactory relationships, but where they do not, we need to be prepared to intervene. We can look for ways in which the child's particular talents can contribute to the work of the class or the group as a whole, and so be recognised and valued by others. We can organise activities which are known to be particularly popular where the friendless child is joined by a small group of other pupils who are keen to take part in the activity itself. We can discuss the situation openly and honestly with the class, and invite some pupils to form a 'Circle of Friends' who will agree to invite the child to join their games, and defend against any unkindness. We can talk with the child and her family and explore ways in which she can lessen the hostility or rejection. A school and a class which set out quite explicitly to create this community ethos and shared responsibility for each other's welfare is an environment in which problems with relationships can be resolved.

The relationship between child and teacher is equally important. Teaching is a skilled activity which requires a combination of training, ability and experience. However, at any moment teachers can find themselves faced with professional challenges for which their training and experience may not have been sufficient. This may well be the case where children present extreme demands in their learning or in their social relationships. It can also happen when a child's capacity to learn is way beyond that which is expected. In such situations teachers may feel inadequate and threatened.

The child who openly and repeatedly challenges the knowledge and competence of a teacher is unlikely to endear herself, however much that teacher tries to remain sympathetic. It is not always possible to *like* everything about one's pupils, but it is possible and essential to show professional concern for every child's welfare and development. When a child challenges a teacher's expertise their behaviour is often based on a determination to establish facts, not on a desire to make the teacher look foolish. The teacher should respond firmly, acknowledge the right to question and recognise the possibility that anyone can make mistakes. By so doing the child is then encouraged to see that learning is a shared enterprise, and to believe that her own contributions will be accepted and taken seriously.

'Please Miss, shouldn't that be a six?'

Developing an appropriate self-concept and establishing positive attitudes to learning

Confidence in oneself as a learner grows not only through the personal appreciation of one's efforts but through the acknowledgement of those efforts by significant others. Success in school is not always easy to ensure. Some children, particularly those who find difficulty with the early stages of learning to read and write, quickly lose confidence in themselves as potential 'learners'. One often hears such children, even very young ones, say, 'I'm no good at drawing', 'I can't do sums' or 'I don't write nicely'. It is as if they believe their current difficulties to be inherent disabilities, impossible to overcome. They seem to think that they will never be able to draw or write or do sums because of some innate weakness.

Talented and very able children will not usually face this particular problem. They may in fact find the acquisition of skills and the understanding of tasks all too easy. Continuous experience of success can accustom children to believe that this is their right. By finding they can do all that is asked without much effort, such children are in danger of developing an unrealistic sense of their own capabilities, a super-inflated confidence, which will be just as counter-productive to future learning as a lack of confidence. On the other hand, children who find that their unusual learning abilities and talents create hostile responses from others, may steadily lose whatever confidence they originally possessed and begin to devalue themselves as learners.

For some children the constant need to maintain high level performance at all times and throughout their school career can be an unwelcome burden. 'What worries me,' I said, turning over page after page of Emma's work, 'is that you don't appear to have a single grade lower than an A. How would you feel if you were handed back something which was rated a mere B, or even a C?' 'Terrible,' said Emma, 'really awful. I'd feel I'd failed. I think I'd be ashamed or something, I'd have let myself down. I'd try and work twice as hard next time.' Emma spent hours each night on her homework, setting herself almost impossibly high standards. She would rewrite essays if there was so much as a spelling mistake on a page. She withdrew from a tutorial class offered to pupils whom their teachers believed would benefit from some additional intellectual challenge, for fear that missing a normal class for one hour a week might affect her marks. Emma needed the constant reaffirmation of her 'A'-grade rating.

Young people can become high level performers in various ways. A few may be such rapid learners and able thinkers that they find it easy to produce high quality work. For some, teachers' expectations of their abilities may be too low, and the work they set fails to challenge. But for others their performance is due to sheer hard work and a high level of motivation. Constant expectation of high level performance may create a state of continuous stress for the child. The belief in themselves as 'high performers' becomes embedded in their very self-concept, part of their fundamental '*me*'. To be faced with evidence that suggests otherwise is an attack on their sense of self and produces a feeling of dismay. Children find it very difficult to separate themselves from the outcomes of their efforts. They cannot see that the inability to solve a problem depends as much on the nature of the problem as on the ability of the person attempting to resolve it. They believe that succeeding makes you worth more, and failing makes you less. This is one of the reasons why youngsters will often refuse to have a go at something they recognise as being difficult.

For the high performing pupil the problem becomes more acute as each year passes. For those who achieve their record through hard work and high levels of motivation the increasing demands of the secondary school curriculum pose a very real threat. In reality only the most outstanding will manage to sustain top-line performance through-out their school career. Some may accept this fact with equanimity, others may not. These are the ones who are likely to become obsessed with marks as a constant reaffirmation of their standing.

Children need opportunities to experience success in order to gain in self-confidence, but they also need opportunities to take risks, and even to fail. We learn as much from our failures as we do from our successes. Unfortunately, many very able and talented children grow up to fear failure. They often become increasingly reluctant as they grow older to take any action which involves a risk. The seeds of this reluctance are

sown in the primary years. If a child grows to believe that her intelligence is her main, and perhaps her only, asset, then the need to cling on to a belief in her intellectual superiority assumes a disproportionate importance. If a child only feels safe as a person when acknowledged as being an 'excellent' performer, she will take care not to declare herself in any way unless she can be sure of achieving such excellence. This need to be a top performer at all times can, if teachers and parents are not careful, become truly burdensome. We have to help children understand that only by having the courage to take risks will we ever discover our full capabilities. Just as a gymnast has to risk falling off the apparatus if she is to master a sequence of movements, anyone who wants to improve their performance has to be willing to take risks, and accept the failures as part of their essential training.

What can be done to help such young people relax their hold on such a punishing and distorting self-image? We need to help children to develop a healthy, positive and realistic appreciation of themselves, and to establish good working habits, however difficult or easy they find it to learn. We need to make sure we do not allow them from an early age to become locked into the trammels of unrelenting success. We need to make sure that we provide learning situations where achievement is not measured in traditional ways, where the taking part, the effort given and the contribution that one makes to the learning of others is recognised and valued. We need to base more of their learning on open-ended approaches which allow them to pursue their enquiries in a variety of ways, including access to the world of learning through the use of information and communication technology so they are constantly aware of how much more there is to know. And we need to engage them in planning and assessing their own learning.

Chapter 6

School organisation and provision

Education is not the filling of a pail but the lighting of a fire.

W. B. Yeats

Recognising and assessing abilities

If we are to provide suitable learning experiences for pupils we need to assess what they know, understand and can do as a basis for any educational planning. The process should consider their academic needs as well as their social and emotional development.

It has always been difficult to agree on what we understand by 'ability', and in particular what we mean when we say a child has 'exceptional' ability or talent. Human ability and human performance are not uni-dimensional. Way back in the 1970s Eric Ogilvie, who wrote extensively about high ability, proposed six categories of 'giftedness': physical talent, artistic talent, mechanical ingenuity, leadership, high intelligence, and creativity (Ogilvie 1973). Since then other models have been proposed, one of the most influential of which is that of Howard Gardner, professor of Neurology at Boston University School of Medicine. He concluded that we have seven intelligences: Linguistic (the ability to use language), Logical and Mathematical (the ability to reason, calculate, and think logically), Visual-spatial (the ability to paint, draw and sculpt), Musical (the ability to compose, play an instrument and sing), Bodily-kinesthetic (the ability to use hands and body), Inter-personal (the ability to relate well to others), and Intra-personal (the ability to know oneself). According to Gardner, our ability to understand and make sense of the world requires the use of all seven intelligences (Gardner 1993). Each kind of intelligence is likely to generate its own form of creativity, and therefore is able to be recognised for itself. Exceptional ability can thereby be defined as a level of ability in a particular sphere of activity, which is unusual in terms of its quality or level of performance for the population in which it occurs. A person can demonstrate unusual levels of ability in *all* areas of their development, or in any one sphere.

Parkyn, a New Zealand psychologist, provided yet another perspective. He suggested two major dimensions to the development of exceptional ability: Precocity, and Intensity (Parkyn 1948). In the early years from birth to five years old 'exceptional' children's development can be described as precocious. They do the same things that all children do, but much earlier, and it is the *early* acquisition of skills that surprises us. They may reach the expected developmental milestones of sitting, standing, walking, saying their first words much sooner than we anticipate and, like little Katie, acquire a level of skill in their exploration, their play and their language which is not often seen at that particular age. Parkyn suggests that from the age of five onwards the development of children with exceptional abilities is not only characterised by its precocity, but by the way the children operate. They may do things in unusual ways, look for interesting and novel solutions, find links between ideas and activities which others have not considered, deliberately choose complex ways of doing things. Their ability to use language in creative and surprising ways may bring a distinctive quality to their writing. Their approach to work and play may be noticeable by its intensity, its heightened sense of purpose and its pursuit of perfection.

It is clearly easier to recognise high ability in whatever form it might manifest itself, if children show this precocious development, or this high level, intense and unusual response through their approach to their work. For such children recognising their abilities is not a problem. There would never have been any doubts, for instance, about the outstanding abilities and potential of such people as John Stuart Mill, Maurice Galton and William Hamilton. Mill studied Greek at the age of 3; by the time he was 4 he was reading classical work fluently, was studying physics and chemistry at a theoretical level before he was 11 and had written two essays on political economy by the age of 16. Galton in the early 19th century was also competent in Latin by the age of 4 and had read the Iliad and the Odyssey by the age of 6. He then turned his attention to physics and chemistry, and by 13 had designed a flying machine. Hamilton was reading Latin, Greek and Hebrew by the age of 5 and could recite long passages of Homer and Milton; he added a new language each year and by the age of 13 had a competent grasp of 13 languages, including Sanskrit and Persian. Recognising their talents would not have been the major concern for Mill's, Galton's and Hamilton's teachers! These men were geniuses, whose extraordinary intellectual ability was only too apparent from the earliest age.

There have always been a few individuals whose development has been so exceptional that we can only wonder at the extraordinary capacity and range of human intellect. Few of us, however, will encounter such people, or be charged with the responsibility for their education and upbringing. But many of us will be involved in one way or another with children who have the potential for exceptional attainment, in the field of academic study, sport or the creative arts. We are also likely to be involved with children who are unable or unwilling to show their potential talents, who do not perform well on the tests we give them, who have lost interest in their work or have chosen to mask their abilities in order to keep in with the crowd. Einstein was by all accounts an indifferent student during his school years, as were many other people who later made outstanding contributions in their own field of work.

So how can we best recognise and assess children's abilities? Children will only be able to demonstrate their talents if they are provided with the opportunities and means to do so. No child became a violinist without being given a violin. We cannot be sure that Stephen Hawking's extraordinary abilities would have been recognised had he been disabled from birth or not been given access to the technology that has allowed him to share his knowledge with the world. If we want to be sure we remain alert to all the evidence that is available we need to adopt an eclectic approach, while recognising that any one approach will have its limitations. Testing, for instance, may provide important information but will not necessarily reliably assess the abilities of individual children. In the past, time and effort has been given to attempts to define what is meant by intelligence and to devising complex ways of testing for its presence using such instruments as IQ tests. Intelligence tests offer a limited perspective on ability, since they are based on a concept of intelligence which is focussed primarily on intellectual, academic ability, which is culturally defined. By defining a person's ability through a numerical score such tests do little more than indicate a person's level of knowledge and reasoning ability in relation to others of the same age. They also have the disadvantage of encouraging unhelpful ways of thinking about a child, and of setting up expectations which may not be in the child's best interest. It is one thing to know what scores children have achieved on tests designed to assess particular aspects of knowledge and skill. It is quite another to understand their individual needs and circumstances. 'An intelligence quotient may be of provisional value as a first crude approximation when the mental level of an individual is sought,' said the psychologist William Stern, writing in 1938, 'but whoever imagines that in determining this quality he has summed up the intelligence of an individual once and for all, leaves off where psychology should begin.'

Tests of any kind can only provide information on those aspects of human performance they are designed to assess, and they will always be subject to factors which affect their reliability. They depend on the willingness of the child to respond. At best they can only ever be an estimate of what a person can do. However such 'estimates' can be useful if they are used to raise awareness of a potential need for special attention. It is becoming increasingly common for schools to use the information obtained from tests such as the Standard Assessment Tasks (SATs) and other formal assessments to identify pupils with particularly high as well as those with very low attainments. In addition, some schools use other standardised assessments of linguistic, numerical and non-verbal reasoning ability which can identify children whose performance is well above that of their peers.

However, teacher observation is equally important. We need to be alert to the information children may be conveying to us through their work, play and behaviour.

Matthew, aged 6, introducing movement and perspective into his drawings

Metamorphosis of Narcissus

> (Poem based on the Salvador Dali Painting by Ruth Larbey, aged 10)
>
> Nimbus clouds whisping about in a great turmoil of action.
> A pond with no movement breaking the thin film-like surface.
> The sun rising above the jagged mountains in the far distance
> in a land where all things mythical and real live together in perfect
> harmony.
> In a land where the sun and the moon come together to paint the sky
> the most amazing colours and hues.
> Now, in the world of change, a great feat.
> The great god Narcissus is stirred to finally waken from his deep slumber.
> Out of the pond and into the wide world, metamorphosis takes place,
> and into man form he changes,
> And there in the cave of fantasy he dwells ad infinitum.

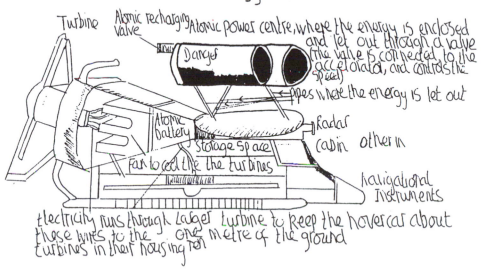

A car running off atomic power

The atomic atoms in the contain cannot escape as it is surraund by an compound called ub 72 which when dented will not let the energy escape and can not be cracked

Turbine

Atomic recharging valve

Atomic power centre, where the energy is enclosed and let out through a valve (the valve is connected to the accelorator, and controls the speed)

Danger

pipes where the energy is let out

Atomic battery

Radar

cabin

other in

Storage space

Fan to cool the the turbines

navigational Instruments

Electricity runs through Larger turbine to keep the hovercar about these wires to the one metre of the ground turbines in their housing ten

However, because not all children's talents show themselves in traditional ways, we also need to be alert to other clues. Checklists of other indicators such as the ones provided in the appendix section can be useful in raising questions in our minds. Most important of all, we are most likely to discover what children are capable of if we give them the right opportunities to demonstrate their talents. No-one will find out how high a child can jump unless the bar is systematically raised and all children are encouraged to exert themselves to the limit. We will never know what children can do with their minds unless they have opportunities that stretch their thinking muscles.

So, with a judicious balance of formal assessments, sensitive observation and broad-based information gathering, within a context of a challenging learning environment, it should be possible to establish a clear picture of a child's abilities on which to plan an educational programme.

Establishing a whole-school policy

The great majority of schools have a policy on equal opportunities which include statements regarding the rights of all children, including the most able, to an education which is broad and balanced and meets their individual needs. The main purpose of a policy is to set a context for the school's work, to make explicit the school's aims and objectives against which the quality of its work and its provision can be judged, and to help all members of the community to reach common understandings and agreements about the attitudes, values, and practice, which will characterise the school's provision.

Current legislation does not include pupils with exceptional ability within the category of pupils who have special educational needs. In fact, there is no legal requirement or expectation that schools should have a policy for more able pupils. Nevertheless, some schools have chosen to include reference to very able children within their whole-school and departmental special needs policies. In many ways it makes sense to do so. A number of schools have already changed the terms for describing the additional support they offer from 'special' to 'individual'. They have an 'Individual Needs' department, with an Individual Needs coordinator. This makes the inclusion of children with unusual or exceptional ability among those considered to have special needs much easier. However, whether the needs of these children are included in the school's 'equal opportunities' policy, or in the special/individual needs policy, the school should set out clearly and in detail what arrangements will be made to meet their needs. It must also establish roles and responsibilities, especially if, as with children with special needs, the children's progress and welfare is to be appropriately monitored and the school's arrangements and any special initiative evaluated. The National Association for Able Children in Education (NACE) has a range of useful booklets on drawing up policies for very able children. Other helpful guidelines are provided in Deborah Eyre's 1997 book, *Able Children in Ordinary Schools,* and in the Cheshire Management Guidelines.

Curriculum planning

Planning to meet the needs of very able children within the context of mixed-ability classrooms, or even in classes which have been set by ability, is not always easy, especially if there is one child whose understanding and skill far outstrips that of the rest of the class. Teachers have to ensure that the tasks they present children do in fact challenge their thinking, and encourage them to produce work which extends their existing knowledge and skills. If work is set at the same

'I don't care about your advanced computer course, Richard, we've still got a test on the three-times table this morning'

level for the whole class, some children may struggle and lose confidence, while others may become bored and frustrated or learn to reduce their effort and output.

Teaching is a highly skilled and demanding activity, and in recent years teachers have been hard-pressed by the many changes and developments they have been required to introduce to their classrooms. Nevertheless, with care and imagination, appropriate and relevant learning opportunities can be planned for the great majority of children with exceptional abilities within the context of their regular classrooms.

The National Curriculum has established an overall framework for children's learning. By setting out the levels of knowledge, skills and understanding children can acquire at different stages of their learning in all subjects in the curriculum, the National Curriculum provides a 'map' which schools and teachers can use when planning for pupils in different age ranges or at different stages in the learning. This makes it easier for teachers to provide for children with precocious levels of attainment, since the higher levels of working have been set out in some detail, providing teachers with a clear indication of what children can be expected to achieve. However, just moving children ever onwards and upwards through the identified levels of learning is insufficient as the sole means of providing learning experiences. It is also a fairly crude approach to planning and managing the curriculum. It can create major organisational difficulties as a child progresses through the educational system.

Other more imaginative and sensitive approaches can be incorporated within the National Curriculum framework. There are now a number of textbooks and handbooks which provide practical advice for planning for very able pupils in ways which are manageable within the classroom. Among the best are *Able Children in Ordinary Schools* (Eyre 1997), *The Challenge of the Able Child* (George 1997), *Accelerated Learning* (Smith 1996) and the Cheshire Management Guidelines, already cited. It is not within the scope of this book to provide extensive detail on classroom provision and teaching strategies which have been so comprehensively described elsewhere (see reference section). However, it is worth highlighting two approaches which have been found to be particularly effective by teachers when planning for a range of levels of challenge in any classroom activity.

The first is Bloom's Taxonomy. Bloom identified characteristics of different levels of thinking which he placed in a hierarchical order from the simplest to the most complex and demanding (Bloom 1956). The six levels are: Knowledge, Comprehension, Application, Analysis, Synthesis, and Evaluation. Thus he proposed that the ability to acquire, understand and use information (Knowledge, Comprehension and Application) are lower-order skills. Analysis (the ability to see patterns, identify components and recognise meanings), Synthesis (generalising from given facts, relating knowledge from several areas, predicting and drawing conclusions) and Evaluation (comparing, discriminating and assessing) are higher-order skills and are more intellectually demanding.

Bloom's Taxonomy

KNOWLEDGE:	Facts, Figures, Information, Observation, Recall,...
COMPREHENSION:	Understanding, Interpreting, Comparing, Contrasting, Ordering,...
APPLICATION:	Using knowledge, method, concepts, Solving problems,...
ANALYSIS:	Recognising patterns, components, hidden meanings,...
SYNTHESIS:	Relating, Generalising, Combining, Predicting, Concluding,...
EVALUATION:	Comparing, Discriminating, Prioritising, Verifying, Assessing,...

Bloom's ideas have been successfully adapted for use in classrooms and for planning different levels of intellectual challenge within individual activities. Using the structure teachers can plan for:

- Different levels of challenge *within* each category (requiring from some children more knowledge, more specialised knowledge, deeper understanding, more examples, further ways of applying the knowledge, new patterns, more detailed analysis, more varied or more complex ways of relating ideas, broader or more interesting ways of comparing, assessing, evaluating).

- Giving different *emphasis* or weight to particular categories according to different needs and abilities (requiring some pupils to spend more time on analysis, synthesis or evaluation of the core task, on the assumption that mastery of knowledge and comprehension will have been more easily acquired).

- Allocating aspects of tasks which require different levels of challenge to particular pupils (when pupils are engaged in a group activity which involves a variety of tasks, some may undertake those aspects which require higher-order thinking skills, such as researching, assessing or prioritising information, while others may contribute through more practical ways).

Using Bloom's Taxonomy to plan a learning task

Planning for a topic on plants	
Knowledge:	– Name the plant
Comprehension:	– What does each part do?
Application:	– Compare shape, size, colour of plants
Analysis:	– Why are seeds that shape? (seed dispersal, pollination)
Synthesis:	– Design a plant for different locations
Evaluation:	– Which plant will grow best in particular conditions, locations?

A chart for planning questions and tasks based on Bloom's Taxonomy is provided in Appendix B.

The second is based on an approach to planning for different needs within the classroom proposed by Brahm Norwich 1996. Norwich suggests teachers consider the learning needs of children in terms of three categories: *common* needs (those that affect all the pupils), *exceptional* needs (those that affect particular groups of pupils, such as those with literacy difficulties, with hearing impairment etc.), and *individual* needs (those that are special to a particular pupil, such as a child who is traumatised by a home circumstance, or a child who requires a special piece of equipment).

Using this approach teachers can plan tasks for groups of children and for individuals using a structure of: MUST, SHOULD, COULD. If, to avoid confusion, the term 'exceptional' is replaced by the term 'additional', very able children might be grouped within the categories of *common* needs and *additional* needs, whereas a child with exceptional ability might be considered to have *common* needs and *individual* needs. So, in deciding what activities the class would carry out during the study of a particular topic the teacher might expect that *all* the class

'Must'… (learn the names, study, record, list, write…); *some* children 'Should'… (practise, work on more examples, write a more extensive account…); and *certain* children 'Could'… (research, seek alternatives, review…). A model such as this allows for flexibility to be readily incorporated into all planning, and enables interesting and challenging activities to be offered to children with a very wide range of abilities.

Planning for differentiated activities for a topic on homes (Gwen Goodhew)

Topic on homes		
Must	Should	Could
Look at local homes	Find local examples of different house types	Compare local houses, analyse features. Compare costs, evaluate market values
Talk about differences	Use technical terms: high-rise, tenement, detached/semi-detached, council, flats…	Find homes suitable for old people, single people, families. Explain why.
Collect, draw pictures	Observe different styles at different historical periods	Explore/research architectural features in different historical periods

Developing children's thinking

While the National Curriculum may provide a useful framework for planning the curriculum, it is the way that teachers work with their pupils that determines how children progress and how effective they become as learners. With a heavy programme of work to cover, and so much emphasis given to knowledge and content in the curriculum, there is a very real risk that natural curiosity will be stifled early in their school career, and that children will become accustomed to being 'receivers', rather than 'active participants'. If we want children to develop lively enquiring minds, to question, reflect, discriminate, judge, and make well informed decisions, we need to help them develop the necessary 'tools'. We need to provide them with the skills for thinking, researching, and solving problems.

For children with exceptional abilities a skills-based approach to learning is of special value, since they often acquire knowledge at a rapid rate, but may not be able to organise and apply their learning in efficient and effective ways. Specific teaching of research skills and approaches to problem solving provides the structures through which children develop greater independence and autonomy, and frees them to work at a pace and at a level that best suits their abilities. Activities can be structured to call upon higher-order skills, as was illustrated through the use of Bloom's Taxonomy. Other approaches can also train children to extend and stretch their thinking muscles and broaden the base of their existing experience. De Bono's 1973 Cort Thinking programme provides a set of thinking and discussion exercises which encourage pupils to think more creatively, imaginatively and logically. Using a snappy set of acronyms (CAF: Consider All Factors; PMI: Plus, Minus, Interesting; C&S: Consequences and Sequels, etc.) the exercises present children with topics for discussion which force them to look beyond the first response and encourage them to avoid being trapped in narrow ways of viewing events. They have mainly been used with older pupils in secondary schools, but can just as effectively be introduced to younger children. They are fun to practise, and once children become familiar with the strategies they can readily and rapidly apply them at relevant moments in a discussion or in planning and reviewing work.

Other approaches such as the development and adaptation of the American-based programme *Philosophy for Children* introduced into this country by Karen Murris 1992, and by Robert Fisher 1995, at Brunel University, have resulted in some highly promising work in a number of schools. The *Thinking Skills* materials and the philosophy and practice that underpin the *Community of Enquiry* approach to learning, described by these two authors, have particular potential for children who want to explore at a high level but who need to learn to appreciate the thinking, contribution and aspirations of others.

Pupil grouping

Until recently it has not been common practice in primary schools in the maintained sector to group pupils by ability, or where some grouping did take place, it was not for all or the majority of their activities. With the advent of the National Curriculum, the increasing emphasis given to pupil attainment and the publication of comparative data, many schools have begun to introduce ability grouping through setting and even streaming. For children with exceptional abilities the changes bring both advantages and drawbacks. On the one hand there may be more opportunities to work with pupils of similar abilities, where ideas and common interests can be shared and theories challenged. On the other, opportunities are reduced for learning to work cooperatively with pupils with different skills and talents, and for appreciating that high intelligence is not always the most important factor in achievement. If children are to grow up as well balanced people they need to experience the benefits of being part of a diverse community. Ideally they need both opportunities to work with pupils of similar ability *and* to engage in activities with pupils where ability is not the common or deciding factor.

Children will need to be able to work at their own pace, and to forge ahead where necessary. Special arrangements may be required to enable some children to pursue their learning with others working at similar levels, at least from time to time. Where a child has exceptional abilities in all aspects of their learning and prefers to work and socialise with older pupils, the school and parents may consider moving the child into a higher class. Most commonly, a primary-aged child will

show a precocious level of knowledge and skill in a particular aspect of the curriculum such as maths or science. In such instances it may be helpful to arrange for the child to join an older group for some activities, while providing differentiated learning opportunities for most of the time within the home class.

In secondary schools setting by ability becomes increasingly common as pupils move up the school. While this may enable teachers more readily to provide work which makes differentiated demands on pupils' knowledge and skills, it is not an adequate response, especially for the student with exceptional ability. In any class, however grouped, there will be a range of abilities and needs. Work will always need to be differentiated. For instance, a revolution in the way people access information is taking place which could have a profound effect on the way teachers and schools organise children's learning. The advances in information technology and the increasing use of 'Integrated Learning Systems' which allow pupils to follow an individualised programme, adjusted to their own pace and style, should greatly reduce the problem of managing the learning of pupils with a wide range of needs and abilities. Children as young as three can learn to access the internet and link up with others beyond their own school. Freed from the responsibility for being the main providers and managers of children's knowledge, teachers can spend more time with individual pupils, discussing, analysing and evaluating their work, looking at implications and interests, exploring potential areas for further enquiry. Children are no longer restricted to learning with and from pupils in their own school, or even country. The world suddenly becomes the children's oyster.

Avoiding the 'Lone-ranger' syndrome

Ensuring that all children in the class are meaningfully occupied throughout the period of time that has been planned for an activity requires careful planning and skilful organisation. A teacher unprepared for a child who works much faster than others and who needs very little help with the tasks he is given, may resort to giving the child time-filler activities: another book to read, another exercise, more of the same. This can quickly sap the child's enthusiasm and does little to encourage him to work as hard next time. Alternatively the busy teacher may be only too thankful to be able to send a capable child to work on his own.

If the teacher is not careful such a child may find himself working far too often and for far too long in isolation, and developing a 'lone-ranger on the desert of life' syndrome.

Modern technology, if it is not sensitively managed, can sometimes exacerbate the isolation. A very bright child can become a very lonely child. Ironically, despite the fact that exceptional children may need as much opportunity for personal contact as any other child, if not more, in order to maintain their interest and excitement in learning, they may end up with much less. Two rather serious consequences may follow. By spending so much time working on their own such children may come to regard all learning as a solitary pursuit, instead of what it should be: a shared activity, an exciting process based on communication. By working on their own the children may become increasingly unable to work, or play, with others. The more 'knowledge' they acquire the greater the distance between themselves and their companions, and the greater the difficulty in believing that other children can be sources of interest and pleasure. In fact, when interviewed as young adults, some very able students described the problems they now experience as a result of never having learnt to chat or engage in small talk and never having developed friendships and easy working relationships with children of the same age.

The teacher needs to be aware of these risks and to monitor carefully the amount of time a child spends on independent learning. She will need to create opportunities for paired and group tasks in which different levels of competence can be of value rather than a disruption. Pupils can be paired for research work, and for work on computer programmes. Thematic project work can provide a flexible base for such cooperation between children. Stories need not only be produced by individuals, but can be developed in groups. Activities can be devised which call upon all class members to contribute, which are based on interests rather than dependent on skills, and which highlight the sharing of experiences and the mutuality of feelings. Teachers can organise children into 'Jigsaw' groups, where each member is given a particular aspect of a task to carry out or research and where they come together after an agreed time to produce their group product or findings. Or 'Rainbow' groups, where each group is given a different aspect of a task to work on together. New groups are then formed composed of one child from each original group, and the findings are pooled. In a context where the contribution of each child is important to the group's outcome, the special abilities of very bright children can

be welcomed by their peers, rather than used as a reason to mock.

While time must be found for all children to have individual contact with an adult this does not always have to be with the teacher. A wealth of talent and enthusiasm exists among parents and within the community at large. Many people are happy to give time to meeting with individual or small groups of children. Nowadays most schools welcome the help available from parents, from community volunteers, and from older pupils taking part in work experience or where this forms part of their course work for GCSE, GNVQ or General Studies. Sixth form students can befriend younger pupils, and act as mentors in specialist subjects. Contacts can be arranged with local colleges and universities where students may also be interested in supporting pupils with particular interests. Many a child's continued enthusiasm for learning has been founded on the early provision of such mentors and friends. A school which welcomes the contributions that a whole community can make towards the education and development of its children is in a good position for being able to meet the needs of even the most exceptional children.

Individual education plans

Individual education plans, introduced by the *Code of Practice* 1994, for pupils with special educational needs, have raised awareness about the importance of paying additional attention to the needs and progress of pupils who have difficulties with their learning. They have acted as the catalyst for planning and reviewing the school's arrangements, and for ensuring that there is a coherent approach to any special or additional provision. The structures and procedures provide a suitable way of planning for any pupil for whom flexible arrangements are needed, including pupils who are exceptionally able and talented. An individual education plan can legitimise alternative activities or the involvement of people from outside the school. For instance, arrangements can be set out in the pupil's plan for a child or young person to follow a course of study other than that of their peer group, such as may happen where a secondary-aged pupil is entered early for external examinations or follows an Open University course. Where additional opportunities are made available through the school's extra-curricular programme, these too can be entered as part of the overall provision which will meet an individual pupil's needs. The central tenet in drawing up an individual plan is the involvement of the pupil and the parents in helping identify the child's needs and in agreeing on ways of meeting them. It requires pupils, teachers and parents to set targets and to meet regularly to review progress. Such processes have great potential for raising pupil motivation and encouraging responsibility for their own learning. They also have potential for identifying the resources and sources of support that can be made available if people are prepared to be flexible and creative, and are willing to work together.

Additional opportunities

The formal curriculum provides the platform for teacher planning and pupil learning in the classroom. But the whole school experience provides countless other opportunities for building on, extending and enriching the quality of children's learning. Schools which aim to provide for the diverse range of needs and interests of *all* their pupils try to ensure a degree of choice and flexibility for pupils which supplements the core educational provision. Traditionally, this has been accepted practice for children with special needs or learning difficulties where special programmes may have to be organised to help pupils develop their social skills, or where additional experiences may be provided to encourage their independence. For these pupils additional or alternative teaching arrangements may be made and, in Key Stage 4, courses leading to sources of accreditation other than GCSE are often organised. Such flexibility is equally appropriate for children with exceptional ability. In addition to the normal practice of modifying classroom work, some schools organise tutorial groups, drawing together pupils with similar interests or levels of learning for extension work in particular subjects. Others set up lunch-time and after-school clubs or arrange 'seminar groups' for pupils interested in discussing challenging issues. Other special arrangements include annual competitions for science or technology projects, special 'enrichment' days, or residential courses for advanced specialist work in different subjects. The ethos and the quality of a school is often defined by these 'additional' opportunities which demonstrate a whole community commitment to the development of pupils as individuals as well as promoting their shared needs and interests.

Chapter 7

Special considerations

Acceleration in the early years

For many children with exceptional ability finding a group of pupils with similar abilities to work with will not be easy, especially where a child is working at a level which is three or more years above other children of the same age. When, for instance, Mark was only 6 years old his parents were keen for him to be moved into a class of 8-year-olds, as they believed his naughtiness at home stemmed from boredom and frustration at school. Sometimes moving the child into a higher class for all, or for some of the time, is thought to be the answer, as it was in the case of Mark. He was already working on GCSE level maths problems by the time he was 8, and had established himself very satisfactorily in a class of 10-year-olds. But such a provision required special arrangements that had to be made both within the school and with the school to which he was due to transfer.

'Acceleration' can be used to solve the problem of being intellectually out of line from the peer group, but it has its complications. The needs of the whole child, his or her ability to manage in a class of older children without being at risk of exploitation, and the prospects for the longer term, must be considered most carefully. Short-term solutions may create problems later when, for instance, the acclerated child may have to stay behind at the time of transfer to the secondary school, and friendship groups have to be disrupted. Although acceleration can prove successful and some children will flourish, many people who later speak about their experience report that it made life very difficult for them, especially in the teenage years, and added to their sense of alienation. If possible, it is almost always preferable to find other alternatives, which allow for flexibility in grouping, but do not rely on joining an older class as the main solution.

The issue of acceleration is a contentious one. Above all, the deciding factor must be the welfare of the individual child and her immediate and long-term interests. In the great majority of cases it should be possible to make arrangements in the child's class or school which are sufficiently flexible and which do not distort the child's normal progression through the school phases.

Transition between primary and secondary school

Education is a continuous process. It begins the day we are born, and continues to our life's end. However, within the formal educational system, there are several distinct phases: the preschool or 'nursery school' phase; the infant and junior, or primary years; secondary school; and the wide range of further education opportunities. Such phases, or stages in education, are not necessarily based on predetermined patterns in children's development, nor are they the same even within or across a Local Educational Authority. Although the marking out of Key Stages in education has provided a structure for planning curriculum content, and monitoring children's progress and attainment, there is no common pattern to the organisation of schools in terms of the age range for which they provide. Thus a change of school and a move on to the 'next phase' can take place at almost any age dependent on the organisation of schools in any given area. Children can transfer to different school at the age of 5, 7, 8, 9, 11, 13, 14, or 16. Each arrangement has its merits and its disadvantages but all present new challenges for children.

Pupils in their final year of primary schooling have usually lived within that community for a number of years. They have become familiar, perhaps overfamiliar, with the routines, the cycle of events, the expectations and the demands both within and outside the classroom. They have learned to adjust to the routines of the school and, in turn, expect particular patterns of response from their teachers. In fact school may well have developed a predictability that 10- and 11-year-old children begin to find tedious. During their last year they are encouraged to think ahead, to look forward to the new opportunities, to the increased range of subjects, the more specialised equipment and resources and the greater range of sporting activities they will find in the next stage of education. At the same time, being 'senior members' of the community, they are expected to accept additional responsibilities and remain committed to all that is happening in their present school. This dual focus, with the need to stand at the centre of a seesaw, can create some of the tensions we see emerging at this stage. Some children, of course, respond quite happily to the interests and demands of their special status. Others, particularly those who have already outgrown the primary school environment, may want to demonstrate their developing independence, strength and maturity in ways which their teachers find unhelpful, especially if this entails a rejection of their authority. James, for instance, had always enjoyed school. He was recognised as being very bright, particularly in mathematics, and until Year 6 he had worked hard and seemed happy to take part in class activities. Then there were signs of trouble. He became restless and demanding. He began to play around in class and challenge his teacher. She in turn became increasingly concerned, and irritated by what she perceived to be a waste of the child's energies and talents.

It is also around this time, between the ages of 9 and 13, that significant physical and intellectual changes begin to take place. The onset of puberty not only marks the growth towards physical maturity, it is also linked to an intellectual growth, a significant widening of potential understanding and ability to deal with abstract concepts.

Very bright children may experience increased tension between their own growth patterns. Some bright all-rounders develop physically earlier than most. They become much taller, stronger and more mature-looking than their class companions. They are in consequence treated as being older and expected to behave with greater respon- sibility. They may not respond to these expectations in acceptable ways. The mismatch between themselves and others can be felt acutely and become a source of embarrassment and distress. Such children may respond by trying to become as insignificant as possible, avoiding being marked out in any way. Unable to escape the distinguishing effects of size and physical maturity, they may attempt to reduce attention by playing down their ability, and deliberately reducing the quality of their work. Many very able children, previously excellent and enthusiastic students, disappoint their teachers during this final year. They are thought to be 'failing to live up to their promise'. Teachers may not realise that this is the child's attempt to fit in with the peer group. Other children may react differently. Some may assume leadership roles assigned to them because of their superior size and ability, but not necessarily in ways appreciated by the adult members of the community, or by other pupils.

Not all very bright children show this early growth spurt. Some experience significant intellectual development much earlier than is common, even as young as 7 or 8, but may not grow in size to match. While beginning to think like adolescents, they remain child-sized. They may be unable to cope emotionally with the preoccupations of their minds. There may be a deeply distressing mismatch between their interests and those of their friends, between the kinds of things they want to discuss and the preoccupations of children of their own age. Longing to take part in adult discussions, to discuss the meaning of life, the concept of infinity, the idea of immortality, they may find that no-one is willing to share their concerns.

For these children the transition stages may be more than usually uncomfortable and induce feelings of intense frustration, loneliness, despair and even madness. When this happens children often seek relief by withdrawing into a private world of study, which only increases their sense of isolation. Or, as many parents recount, they look for contact with older children, sometimes aping their ways in a desperate attempt to become accepted and perceived as more mature than they really are.

'A deep strangeness fell upon me, which made me feel all my life a sojourner on this planet rather than a native', wrote Norbert Weiner, who entered high school at the age of 10, alongside fellow students who were 17 years old. Weiner's case is highly unusual, but there are many children who find their unique pattern of development creates real difficulties, particularly at critical stages such as transition.

There are, however, huge age variations in the onset of puberty. As a general trend it is recognised that girls mature earlier than boys, but even within the sexes the differences are considerable. The growth spurt occurs in some children as early as 9 or 10 years, whereas in others it may not even be noticeable until they reach 15 or 16. Two factors in particular have implications for the way the transition stages in primary schools are managed. First, at no stage in their lives will the differences between children be so marked or so significant. Second, the onset of puberty is occurring earlier decade by decade. Whereas the problems of the adolescent stage used to be the concern of the secondary school, they are now reaching back and becoming part of the experience of the primary school as well. This has clear implications for the way educational provision is managed in that final year, if not earlier. Account must clearly be taken of the wide variations in pupils' development and their consequent need for appropriate levels of intellectual challenge and for personal support if they are not to feel alienated and demoralised at this critical stage in their education.

For pupils with exceptional ability the problems may not be different in kind from those already described. But they are likely to differ in degree. For the very bright, being in the top age group may also mean additional restrictions to their intellectual growth. A school may have organised its provision for the very able children with maximum flexibility and creativity, perhaps by allowing for alternative class arrangements or occasional groupings across different age ranges, or through clubs and other interest activities. Until children reach the final year they will always have had the potential opportunity of working with older children at some stage, or mixing with them informally and thereby enjoying the stimulus of intellectual compatibility. Once they reach the last year, however, there will be no older children on hand with whom to share such experiences. Opportunities for growth through sharing and exploring directly with other children will therefore be restricted to those available within the existing class or classes in the school, and these may be insufficient.

Furthermore, a very bright child's level of functioning in a subject may have progressed beyond the competence of the teacher, particularly in such subjects as maths and science. The teacher may be hard put to know how to present interesting and challenging problems which match their ability. When, for instance, James's parents were invited into school to discuss the deterioration in behaviour, his teacher learned that he had done a GCSE maths paper at home for fun, and was reading technical books on astronomy. This would not be an uncommon experience. A study of the issues facing teachers of Year 6 pupils, carried out in a number of Oxfordshire primary schools, reported that many teachers find it difficult to challenge very able pupils in areas of the curriculum where they are not subject specialists (Eyre and Fuller 1993). The problem is especially acute in small schools where teachers have to take responsibility for a number of different subjects, and where there may be less opportunity to develop the knowledge and expertise to teach very bright children.

When parents are in agreement schools sometimes try to solve the problem by arranging an early transfer to the secondary school. The advantage of this is that the child may receive the stimulus and intellectual challenges suited to his ability, and is able to study a wider range of subjects. However, this is by no means a universal solution. For one thing, many exceptional children are not one, but two,

three or even more years ahead of their contemporaries. For another, exceptional ability does not always generalise to all aspects of learning, nor is it necessarily matched by a similar emotional maturity. The interests and feelings of a child who has not yet begun the puberty phase are very different from that of the adolescent. By being placed in a group of older children, a very bright younger child may find himself in a social grouping with which he is unable to cope.

As we have seen, there are no simple solutions nor a single blueprint for managing these situations. But clusters of schools have developed a number of joint strategies to meet particular circumstances and the needs of specific pupils. For instance, cooperation between a family of feeder schools might result in the pooling of talent, expertise and interests of the teachers in order to provide extension studies. Children might be grouped across schools for one session a week during which topics, or additional studies (a foreign language, geology, astronomy or mythology, etc.) could be pursued at greater length or in greater depth than would otherwise be possible in one school on its own. Cooperation might also result in each school offering one or two interest clubs, taking place weekly after school. When several schools combine in this way a wider choice of activities can be offered, dependent on the particular interests and expertise of individual teachers, without the burden becoming excessive on any one school. Activities can be planned to meet different levels of experience and competence, through courses for beginners, intermediate or advanced learners. Pupils can meet with a greater variety of people, and thereby be encouraged by the sharing of interests and the challenge of working with others of similar levels of ability. The talents of teachers can be pooled among a wider community; the gaps in expertise in some areas can be supplemented by skills gained in another.

Wellplanned cooperation between feeder schools and their local secondary school produces even greater benefits. Secondary teachers can help primary colleagues by sharing with them their more specialist experience. They might even be released to take up a limited teaching commitment within the primary school, in order to introduce new ideas and skills and to learn for themselves, so that they might become more aware of the primary philosophy and approach, and more informed about the individual abilities and teaching needs of their future pupils. Such arrangements have been very successful in a number of schools in different parts of the country. Special interest clubs within the secondary school can be open to younger children who are considered able to benefit from the experience. Such cooperation signals to both communities that education is a collective as well as an individual enterprise. It signals that the needs of the individual, however unusual, can be met within a community, providing that goodwill, creative thinking and an open policy exist.

Parental aspirations

As parents it is natural to feel pride and pleasure in our children's achievements. We all want them to do well, and to lead interesting and productive lives. But there is always the risk of investing too much of ourselves in our expectations for their future, of burdening them with our own 'dreams'. Children can sometimes provide for their parents the success or the public esteem that has been lacking in their own lives. They can sometimes compensate for past disappointments, and opportunities missed. This is a very real risk for children who show unusual talent or ability.

Marie, for instance, was a promising musician. She started piano lessons at the age of five, and was soon the star in school concerts. Her mother had also been a talented performer, but had not been able to pursue her career in music due to family difficulties. She was delighted by the emergence of her daughter's gifts and devoted a great deal of time, energy and money to supporting Maria's musical development. When later, as a teenager, the girl no longer wished to spend long hours practising and became increasingly reluctant to carry on with her piano lessons, her mother was intensely disappointed.

When too much store is laid on success and achievement children may feel compelled to achieve and thereby become harnessed to the shackles of success. They may grow to believe that they must succeed to retain the love and affection of their parents. Failure to be outstanding then truly becomes something to be feared. We need to be sure that we understand the difference between the pleasure and pride we feel for the *child*, and the pleasure and pride we take for *ourselves*. The first will support the child, the second can be an unwelcome burden.

Parents may have to work hard to identify which activities belong to them, and which belong to the children. This becomes particularly important when it concerns the activities which involve them as a *family*. Joining a 'club' for clever or talented children is especially liable to provoke such situations. For example, it was clear from an early age that Michael was very bright. He was constantly on the move, developing passionate and sometimes obsessive interests. He read voraciously and spent long hours in his room working on his computer. He sometimes complained that he had no-one to share his interests with. Michael's parents were both pleased and proud that their son was showing such a level of intellectual ability, but they were also somewhat bemused. They joined a local organisation which ran sessions for very able children on a Saturday, and greatly enjoyed the social opportunities and moral support this offered them. When Michael lost interest in attending, his parents initially felt deprived of an important focus in their lives. Later, once they had been able to sort out the difference between what Michael wanted and what they needed for themselves, they decided to continue to attend the sessions as volunteer helpers.

Of course, for many children, such organisations provide a lifeline, a real source of support, an opportunity to meet with others of similar interests and to explore personal hobbies in an atmosphere of enthusiasm and delight. The challenge for parents is to see their children as unique individuals with a development and personality all of their own, to have the courage and sensitivity to balance the need to provide encouragement but not to allow personal needs to distort the natural inclinations and pursuits of the child.

Parental support

Good schools actively encourage the involvement of parents in their child's education and the life and work of the school. They see parents as their most important and most valued partners in an enterprise in which many people have a part to play. After all, for most children, parents are the one 'constant' factor in their lives; teachers come and go, others contribute at different times along the way, but parents accompany them throughout their journey through school. Parents have knowledge and experience of their child as they are at home; teachers have knowledge and experience of the child in school. Without an opportunity to share this knowledge and experience both may overlook important factors in the child's development, and fail to take account of things which could help them in their respective responsibilities.

Fortunately the importance of partnership with parents has been given increasing emphasis by schools in recent years, particularly where special consideration has to be given to a child's needs. The guidance offered in the *Code of Practice* 1994, for children with special needs, provides a clear structure for the close involvement of parents in planning and reviewing their child's progress. For children with Statements of special educational need this involvement is mandatory. The development of individual education plans (IEPs) supports this process, since the special or additional arrangements for giving additional help to the child and the responsibilities of everyone who will be involved, including parents, have to be set out in some detail. This would appear to be a most helpful and appropriate way to plan for any child who is thought to need 'special' attention, and could easily be adopted as the process for involving parents of children with exceptional abilities.

Bringing up a child is not easy. We have to not only see ourselves as partners, but respect each other's particular experience of the child, recognise our different roles and responsibilities, and treat each other with sensitivity. We must find the time and the setting which will encourage a meaningful sharing of information and expectations, and reduces the risk of a one-way traffic of communication.

Chapter 8

Surviving adolescence

Conflicting demands

In England, we have a culture which does not always value academic success. Ask anyone what their mental image of a very clever child looks like, and likely as not they will come up with a version of a 'nerd' or a boffin, a poor physical specimen, with heavy glasses and eyes weakened through excessive study, and spindly limbs due to lack of healthy exercise. Across the country we have a very real problem of underachievement, particularly among boys. In far too many schools it is not 'cool' to be clever.

Take this description from one boy's science teacher:

Martin is a walking disaster. He seems to live in a world of his own. He is never where he should be. If he ever does turn up to the right lesson he is invariably late. He really doesn't seem to know whether he's coming or going. As for his work, it is quite disgraceful. He is extremely reluctant to put anything down on paper, and quite honestly, when he does it's so untidy, so carelessly done that I quite often refuse to mark it. And yet . . . and yet there's something about the lad that makes me wonder. When he does get interested in what we're doing he asks the most extraordinary questions. Really intelligent and perceptive ones. He often seems to see the solution to a problem before others have even understood the question and he enjoys looking for alternative ways of reaching a conclusion. In fact, when he stops playing the class clown he can be really quite profound.

Then there was Joanna:

She's a model pupil. Her work is quite outstanding. Her particular interest seems to be in history, but she is without doubt the most able mathematician in her year, and she is going to be something of a linguist too. She's such a pleasure to have in the class. She's very popular of course, she's so mature, a born leader.

There is no guarantee that the potential shown by children in the primary years will continue and develop throughout their school career. Excellence in performance requires not only talent and ability but commitment, determination and a willingness to put in enormous amounts of effort. It is somehow easier to accept the truth of this assertion when we consider that it takes talent plus exceptional hard work and practice to become an outstanding athlete, musician or dancer. We tend not to think the same holds true for performing at the highest academic level. It is as if we want to think that if we are 'clever', success will always come easy. But this is very rarely the case. No-one reaches the top of their chosen field simply by having talent. Studies of people who have become outstanding performers almost invariably show that the common factor in all their lives has been a high degree of motivation, an ability to dedicate themselves to reaching a goal, a willingness to put in hours and hours of sheer hard work, and support from their families (Freeman *et al.* 1995; Howe 1996). To achieve at a very high level is rather like baking a cake: you need the basic ingredients of above average ability, high motivation, and favourable circumstances.

The problem is that for young people in our western society, learning and study requirements become more onerous and demanding at the very time in their personal development when they have other more interesting and important preoccupations. They are entering the stage of their lives we call adolescence.

Adolescence is a time in young people's lives which can be fraught with tensions, emotions and anxieties. It is a period when a young person has to move on and outwards from the child who they were, defined in part by their parents and their environment, to become a person created in their own terms. This exciting but troubling process of discovering and defining a new self involves a drawing away from one's parents and other familiar adults, a growing acceptance of a new physical self, and the management of powerful and troubling emotions. A useful way of understanding what happens during this 'transformation' phase of life has been put forward by the psychologist W. D. Wall. He wrote about the young person embarking on the task of constructing four distinct but intricately related selves: a sexual self, a social self, a vocational self, and a philosophical/moral self (Wall 1968). The development of these various aspects of himself in order to build a new and separate adult identity will inevitably involve the young person in an extended period of experimentation and readjustment and growth, both within himself and in the context of his relationships with others.

First, there are quite obvious and quite unavoidable physiological developments: the body expands, upwards and outwards, often at a sudden and alarming rate; facial features become transformed, bodily shape alters, hair appears on previously smooth parts of the anatomy, bulges emerge, skin takes on a different quality and texture. These changes, accompanied as they are by hormonal developments affecting sensation and mood, are simultaneously intensely fascinating and a source of anxiety and apprehension. Imagine how we would feel as adults, if a similar re-shaping of our features and body structure were suddenly to take place. In the normal course of events these bodily changes and developments begin at around the time that significant intellectual growth occurs. The young person's ability to view events only from his own perspective, to consider the world only in relation to his own experience, expands into an ability to transcend his own immediate thoughts and to consider many possible points of view. Two significant things follow as a result. The young person becomes able to turn his eyes upon himself, from the outside, as it were, seeing himself as others might see him, and he becomes capable of thinking about the nature of thought, of holding a number of possible hypotheses at once and reasoning between them. He learns to 'play' with ideas. The initial experiences are understandably both exciting and alarming. Being able to turn one's own eyes upon oneself carries with it the discomfort of seeing, or imagining, the blemishes as well as the beauties. Finding that one's body is behaving in such unpredictable, and not always welcome, ways can cause embarrassment and anxiety. It also faces the young person with the pain of acknowledging the gap that exists between what is the reality and what is the dream.

Much of the adolescent obsession with the reflection in the mirror, the excessive self-admiration and the excessive self-criticism, is based on the need to adjust to the new emerging self, and to come to terms with what is happening. It is also to do with the fact that this is an intermediary period, where the differentiation of oneself from others, of

The pain of acknowledging the gap between the reality and the dream

one's thoughts from the opinions of others , is not fully realised. It is a period of great imbalance. The young person, able to see himself from the outside and to reflect upon his own thoughts, finds himself fascinating and imagines everyone else must do so too. Everything he admires about himself must be admired by others, any perceived blemish must be equally despised. The disparities between the realities of the present and his dreams for the future may result in feelings of resentment towards a world which is so obviously determined to thwart the realisation of his ideals.

   The new-found ability to juggle with ideas encourages a state of indecisiveness which often infuriates adults, and drives the young person to seek support from his peers. It is the time of peer group bonding, of 'us against the world', where the approval of one's friends is far more important than that of adults. Together they can complain about the ignorance of the adult world, and construct their own imaginary El Dorado. All things become possible because solutions can always be found in the endlessly creative mind.

For young people whose development is out of line with their peers, or who cannot find a peer group to which they feel they belong, this can be a time of great stress. Their ability to look critically at the world and the people within it, and to weigh up the differences between the 'actual' and the 'ideal', may far outstrip their emotional ability to cope with their new ways of thinking. While many children with exceptional ability do achieve a happy balance between their intellectual and social development, some do not.

Martin and Joanna provide striking examples. The problems they were facing were not unique or particularly unusual. To a great extent they were similar to problems faced by all young persons at some stage of their development. The only difference between their experience and that of others seemed to be one of intensity, and of timing. Martin, for instance, had begun to ponder on questions of world significance while still at junior school. He had found himself growing increasingly aware of his parents' and his teachers' failings, and angry with what he felt to be gaps in their understanding. While still a child, his intellectual development had leapt ahead, leaving him emotionally bewildered and unhappy. No compensatory physiological changes were taking place at that time to divert his attention. No-one else around seemed to share his experience. He felt truly alone. He wanted to shut his mental eyes and return to the happier unquestioning state he still remembered, but he could not. His thoughts would not allow him to. So began for him the bad period, when he became restless and confused within himself and a puzzle to his family and friends. Later, when he did begin to develop physically, the whole process became unbearable to him. His body betrayed him. It grew large and ugly. His arms and legs developed a life of their own. Martin looked a mess and he hated himself. Gone were the cherished thoughts of himself as the fictional hero. What he saw in the mirror was a travesty of the brilliance of the inner person.

Furthermore, Martin was experiencing great difficulty with the early stages of reading and writing. As a result he was not only frustrated by the betrayal of his physical appearance, but intellectually trapped, unable to give proper expression to his thinking in the ways which were valued in school. He looked a mess. His work looked a mess. He disowned himself. He became a clown. By the time I met Martin he had given up on the world of adults. In his eyes, no-one outside himself was of any worth. No-one, he believed, was able to understand him, share in his interests, or recognise the brilliance and uniqueness of his thoughts. Teachers especially were worthy only of his contempt. Teachers, he said, clearly cared nothing for the real life of their pupils; they had never taken the trouble to get to know *him*. They had always treated him as though he were stupid, whereas it was they, in fact, who were ignorant. Most of the time they would not let him ask questions or express his views because they realised they could not cope with what he wanted to discuss. He knew they had to keep their distance and behave like robots just to keep control. Bitter, disillusioned, Martin was only 13 years old.

Joanna, on the other hand, faced a different kind of problem. She had matured both physically and intellectually at an even pace, but was way ahead of her classmates. Up until the time I met her she had led a charmed life. The elder daughter in a family of two, her parents both teachers, she basked in their loving support. Her father's passionate interest in history soon became her own. Together they visited museums and took part in archaeological digs at weekends. Her mother had a background in modern languages and the family spoke French at meal times. Joanna had always been a loving, sociable child: a source of pride and delight to her parents; a much prized pupil to all her teachers. She had been recognised as being exceptionally bright from a very early age and had been encouraged throughout her school career. Joanna was destined for high academic and social success.

Unlike Martin, Joanna believed in the fundamental honesty of teachers. She too could recognise human failings and the need to keep face at times of challenge. But Joanna sympathised. She said she understood the difficulties. She, like Martin, was often despairingly bored. 'But,' she said, 'it's often my fault. I always read ahead so of course I get bored if we have to go over it all again in class. It must be very difficult for a teacher to have someone in the class like me. After all they have to help all those who take longer to understand. That's only fair.' Joanna was only 12. In many ways she was mature beyond her years. To many, Joanna did not seem to have a problem. But as we discussed her work it became clear that it was fear of adult disapproval that was preventing her from expressing her real feelings of frustration. She had a natural empathy and sensitivity towards the feelings of others and a precocious ability to identify with their experience. She also needed to be always thought of as a 'good' girl, a 'good' student, and this was encouraging her to be over-compliant. Joanna, like Martin, was not well understood by her teachers. The difficulty for Joanna, as she moved into adolescence, would be in exploring her true self, developing her own opinions, and establishing her own identity.

No two youngsters could have been more different from each other than were Martin and Joanna. Yet they shared in common the dilemmas that invariably face all young persons at one time or another. They also shared a special dilemma and a particular confusion in experiencing an adolescence that was precocious and, in Martin's case, unequally balanced. As such it presented them with a personal challenge that was indeed rather special. Their particular paths to maturity were made easier once the adults involved began to recognise the problems, and were willing to help the youngsters develop their special talents more constructively and in ways which reflected their unique identity. This is not always an easy task as it can make heavy demands on one's patience and ingenuity. It demands personal maturity and a willingness to look at relationships with young people with honesty. It means recognising that very bright youngsters may be just as much in need of guidance and personal support as others with more evident difficulties. It certainly requires a thorough examination of the opportunities offered to youngsters within a school's organisation.

The issue of gender

'I well remember making a conscious decision about this when I was fourteen,' said Jenny. We were talking about the difficulties many girls experience in trying to reconcile the fact of being clever *and* feminine. 'It felt like a choice at the time. I sensed it would have to be either one or the other, that I could not, or would certainly not be accepted as being able to be both. Of course I think things have changed now, but I believe a lot of the old prejudices and stereotyping are still around.'

And indeed they are. We have already seen that there are pressures during a child's early life and school career to persuade him or her to conform to expectations and, in the case of clever children, to dissuade them from making their exceptional abilities too obvious. Once children reach secondary age, the pressures become affected by gender expectations. Gender expectation affects both boys and girls and in different ways.

A number of research studies have produced evidence which suggests that there are different patterns of neurological development between boy and girl babies which predispose them to different early development of particular skills and interests. Such studies have also shown that boys and girls may have different rates and types of intellectual (as well as physical) development and that these may have a bearing on their response to and performance in particular subjects. For instance little boys seem to be more interested in play which involves making, doing, and exploring the properties of objects which might lead to a greater propensity for and interest in the practical aspects of maths and science. The greater interest for many little girls in talking, cooperative and social play may lead to their greater advantage in language based activities. (Fox and Zimmerman 1985, Walden and Walkerdine 1985, Freeman 1991).

Whatever the neurophysiological facts about brain development, the belief that the 'capacity' of the female brain is different from that of the male, is unhelpful when it comes to children's development and relationships, as misinterpretation can lead to the information being used in inappropriate ways. It can lead to generalisations which distort people's views of one another and deny the uniqueness of the individual. It is more important to be aware of those factors which influence the way children develop, and make sure that as adults we do nothing that puts limits on children's expectations. If children are allowed to think they are not capable of doing something well they are likely to develop this as a personal 'belief', and to become trapped within the limitations of an unhealthy 'can't do' mythology. 'I'm no good at maths, drawing, games, singing...' The list is endless. But the reality may be that they have never been encouraged to work at and improve the skill.

There are a number of different pressures on girls and boys, particularly in adolescence. They tend to be based on cultural factors and what we deem to be expected 'male' or 'female' qualities and behaviour. Sometimes, qualities which, when attributed to men, are described as strong-mindedness, decisiveness and the ability to persevere are interpreted as domineering, ruthless or obstinate when attributed to women. As a result some girls deliberately choose to subdue their responses to conform to social expectations. Vanessa, for instance, had earned something of a reputation in her class. She had a sharp wit and an ability to go straight to the point. In class discussions she would express her views clearly and concisely, often having effectively dismissed the arguments put by others. She was aware she was thought to be bossy and a know-all. 'Fat chance she has of getting a boyfriend', said fellow students. Carol, on the other hand, chose not to take an active part in class debates. She had to be encouraged to volunteer an opinion. When she did, she measured her words carefully, and tried not to say anything too controversial. Yet beneath her compliant facade Carol was just as aware as Vanessa about the issues and the lack of substance or logic in the arguments presented by her companions. But she preferred to be 'one of the group'. For Carol, the

A choice between being popular and being clever

desire for social success resulted in the denial of her intellectual self. She, like Jenny many years before, had made a choice between being popular, conforming to expectations of her gender, and being clever.

Boys too may be subjected to a number of pressures. While expectations of the role of men have changed significantly in recent years there are still a number of prejudices around, particularly among adolescents. Boys may be mocked if their particular interest or talent does not conform to the still popularly held stereotypes of appropriate 'male' behaviour. We still associate sensitivity and the open expression of feelings with femininity. We encourage this in girls, but in the past we tended to discourage it in boys. The notion of, 'Big boys don't cry', is still around in many families. A sensitive boy, with real insight into creative experience, who wants to dance or write poetry, who responds with emotion to artistic expression, may well have a hard time in many of our schools. His talents and imagination can be crushed and driven out through mockery.

The desire to create an acceptable masculine image for himself can force a choice on a boy as unfortunate and as unnecessary as the one that can face girls. Boys may well be discouraged from following certain courses because to do so would expose them to the embarrassment of being the only boy among a class of girls, or to the mocking remarks of peers.

We also need to take note of research which shows that from earliest childhood families tend to encourage boys more than girls to become independent, self-reliant and able to assume responsibility, the very

qualities that underpin high performance (Fox and Zimmerman 1985). Differences in early encouragement of such qualities almost certainly affect the behaviour and achievements of boys and girls in school. Such family and cultural influences may also lie behind evidence of other differences in children's responses to their work. In a number of studies boys have been shown to be more ready to see their successes as due to their ability, whereas girls tend more often to attribute their success to good luck or the fact that they worked hard, or the task was easy. Boys are more likely to attribute failure at a task to their lack of effort, whereas girls are more likely to attribute failure to a lack of ability (Deaux and Emswiller 1974, Freeman 1991). Girls may also be reluc-tant to attribute success to their ability for fear of seeming to brag, this being thought to be an unattractive trait in girls (Heatherington *et al.* 1989). Girls are also more likely to be praised for their good *behaviour,* whereas boys are more likely to be commended for the quality of their work. If we become more aware of the way social factors and the way our own behaviour affects young people's response to their work, we can take steps to avoid some of the problems before they arise.

Fortunately the gender differences which so badly affected the achieve-ment of so many children in the past seem to be diminishing. Girls have regularly outperformed boys for some time now in areas of the curriculum where they performed less well in the past. For many schools the challenge now is to overcome a culture of underachievement among boys which is just as damaging as the one which used to limit the expectations of girls. But some of the prejudices and stereotypic attitudes remain and can diminish expectations and aspirations of young people. We must continue to watch for those influences which deter any young person from reaching the heights and pursuing paths which are best suited to their talents. Schools can review their own practice and examine their policies to see what they are currently doing, or what they could do, to encourage children's confidence and self-belief. Teachers can examine their own attitudes and behaviour to see whether they are encouraging conformity in girls, but accepting more aggressive and exploratory behaviour in boys. Teachers can help dispel the myth that if you make use of your ability to the full you will be unattractive and actively encourage girls as well as boys to challenge and to be constructively assertive. After all, our teachers can be the role models for the attitudes and values they want to promote. They can regularly and openly discuss the subject of gender roles and stereotyping, and encourage young people to explore their feelings and expectations. They can set high expectations for all pupils and refuse to be satisfied with anything but the best from each individual. They can provide frequent positive feedback which goes beyond the high marks that very able pupils often obtain. Schools can also encourage pupils to take part in out of school activities that introduce them to interests that they may not have previously considered appropriate for their gender. They can enlist the help of parents to make sure they too play their part in encouraging their children to be bold and true to themselves and to value their individuality.

Supporting young people in their work and relationships

Young people need support from adults to help them find a way through some of the challenges they meet in adolescence. But it must be support that recognises their growing maturity and respects their need to find personal solutions to problems. This is not always easy for either parents or teachers, as we are so used to directing and controlling, and to leading children along ways which we believe to be most suitable. Shifting the balance in our relationships so that young people take ownership of their lives and learning during adolescence is one of the great challenges we have to face. We have to guide without imposing, support without taking away the challenge. Tutoring and the use of mentors are among the most effective ways to help pupils through this period.

Tutoring

Staff in schools encourage pupils to take responsibility for their work in many different ways. Records of Achievement, with their emphasis on personal target-setting and review, have made an important contribution in this respect. However, it can be difficult for teachers not to impose their own demands and expectations on pupils. All too often no link is made between the needs for development identified by the pupils and ways in which teachers and the school will help the pupils achieve their targets.

One approach that has proved to be very effective with people of all ages is based on the work of George Kelly and his theory of Personal Constructs. The theory has been used by two psychologists, Laurie Thomas and Sheila Harri-Augstein of Brunel University, to develop 'self-organised learning', a way of helping people become more effective through the use of 'learning conversations'. The approach is called 'Self-Organised Learning'. Thomas and Harri-Augstein argue the need for a language with which to talk about the *process* of learning. We need to learn how to analyse our thinking and our problem solving strategies when we try to absorb new information or develop a new skill. The process involves conversations between a learner and a 'learning coach'. Together they discuss what the learner needs or wants to achieve (the *Purpose)*. They then explore the various ways in which the learner may set about the task (the *Strategies)*. Finally they consider what the learner expects as an outcome and the criteria that will be used to judge success (the *Outcome)* (Thomas and Harri-Augstein 1985).

Central to the approach is the tutor's ability to stay neutral, and avoid putting forward their own solutions, intentions or desires for the learner, for that immediately reduces the learner's ownership and commitment. The coach's role is to explore each of the elements of the learner's plan (purpose, strategy, outcome) and to help him arrive at a course of action. The skill is in making sure that the learner establishes a clear and meaningful purpose, explores a range of possible strategies and chooses one they believe will work, and decides when and how the success will be assessed. In the last part of the process the coach and learner review what has been achieved. After the strategy has been put into operation the learner and coach review not only whether the intended *outcomes* were achieved, but also the appropriateness of each phase of the process.

The value of using such an approach with pupils with exceptional abilities lies in the independence that can be given to pupils in making decisions about how, where, and when, they work. It offers the potential for flexibility, and for sustaining motivation. It also enables a wider group of people to support pupils in their learning; it is not necessary to have specialist subject knowledge to be an effective learning coach.

Mentoring

Mentoring is also becoming popular as a means of additional support. Pupils with exceptional abilities often develop interests that are hard for others to appreciate or share. Their sense of isolation can be exacerbated by the lack of opportunity to discuss their experiences and hobbies. Out in the community there are many people who would enjoy giving time to a young person, and having an opportunity to share common interests. Just as volunteers play an important part in supporting the school's work with pupils with learning difficulties, through hearing children read, accompanying visits and trips and supporting in class, so too can a network of help from the community greatly enhance provision for the most able. Mentors can provide young people with valuable role models, raising their personal expectations, broadening their horizons, introducing them to a wider circle of people with similar interests. Mentors can also provide that invaluable additional personal time which is so difficult for many schools to provide from within their own resources.

Involving the pupils

One of the best ways to find out how to improve the provision we make in schools is to ask the pupils. All too often this valuable source of information is overlooked. We talk to one another, consult with people from outside the school, audit our resources and analyse our results. Only rarely do we go to the consumers themselves and ask them honestly how our provision and practice helps them. We may already ask their opinion about practical things and about extra-curricular activities they might like to have on offer. But, if we want to know how we can help young people learn more effectively we have to be prepared to ask them about the teaching itself and the quality of our personal support. Given the opportunity, young people are usually very helpful and responsive. When staff in one school decided to interview sixth form students about their past experience they found they had to revise a number of assumptions about the school's provision. They asked the students how they learnt best, what prevented them from doing their best work, in what ways the school could help them achieve better, and what changes they would make to alter the situation for pupils who were disaffected. The students emphasised the importance of firm management, high expectations, clear targets, constructive and honest commentary, fair treatment and plenty of opportunities for active participation. They also highlighted their need to work together in groups as well as to be given work to do on their own. Importantly, they identified areas of the school where practice needed attention, and gave constructive suggestions on how to tackle the culture of underachievement among boys. As a result a number of changes were implemented including more opportunities for pupils to take responsibility for their work, homework and extension work clubs and the identification of a member of staff to monitor the progress and provision for high achievers.

Involvement of students in this way has great potential for creating a learning environment which fosters achievement in which everyone feels they have a part to play, and where differences are valued for their contribution to the rich diversity of the community.

Chapter 9

Final words

Looking to the future

The most significant changes that are likely to take place in education over the next few years will be in the use of information technology and the development of interactive, computer-based learning. This may well bring about fundamental changes in the way schools operate, with boundaries between education and training, classrooms and work environments becoming less clear, and divisions between different sectors of education (primary, secondary, tertiary) becoming increasingly blurred (Wood 1993). Such changes are already under way with developments in the 14–19 curriculum and the introduction of courses and qualifications such as GNVQ and NVQ which already cross the secondary/tertiary divide.

The future could look much brighter and easier to manage for children with exceptional ability. The freeing up of classrooms from the traditionally organised, teacher-dependent form of working, to one where students can be released to pursue their enquiries and tailor their pace of learning through the use of modern technology may well bring about the very changes that will resolve the current tensions. The decreased reliance on books, pens and paper as a consequence of laptop computing, communications technology and large scale multi-base databases may well eliminate the source of much current frustration which limits the progress and achievement of so many young people today. Teachers are likely to find themselves spending less time imparting information and testing its reception, and more on providing frameworks for project work and on attending to individual pupil's learning process and progress.

The revolution in communications technology and the move from using computers to access information on an individual basis, to using the technology for group-based work and networking is already under way, at least in some countries. There is clear evidence from the USA that this is the future for education. There are signs that it has already started to happen in the UK and will gather pace in the coming years.

If this is the future, the impact on how young people with exceptional ability are perceived, and how they therefore develop through infancy to adulthood, will be profound. The isolation which has damaged the childhood and adolescence of many young people whose intellectual development and academic interests are out of line from that of their peer group may cease to be the common experience it now is. With different patterns of study being the norm, and the learning environment extending beyond the boundaries of the school and the classroom, young people will be free to establish friendships and working relationships not restricted by a class group or age-related groupings. With less anxiety and concern about *how* their learning needs are to be handled parents and teachers will have more time and energy to concentrate on the relationships we need to build with one another, and on fostering those opportunities and links which underpin the quality of our lives together.

Creating a climate for growth

Growing up is a fascinating process, full of excitements, and possibilities. Living and working with children with exceptional abilities is a privilege. But it has its challenges!

It is challenging for the children themselves because they have to learn to accept themselves as they are, to live with the differences they perceive between themselves and others, to have the courage to be creative, to take risks, to respect and value the talents and contributions of others and to remain optimistic and positive about their relationships with their peers.

It is challenging for parents. They have to provide an environment in which the children feel secure, where the rights of all family members are respected and the needs and demands of one do not override the concern for others, where the interests and abilities of the exceptional child are adequately supported but where the hopes and aspirations of the adults do not become a burden.

It is challenging for teachers and schools. They have to recognise that all children, including the most able, have a right to experiences that enable them to progress, to work at their own pace and have their talents and abilities properly taken into account.

It is challenging for all of us to manage our relationships and our response to one another in ways which are constructive and encourage trust. To ensure that children grow up healthily we need to create the kind of nurturing environments which help children, like plants, develop sturdy roots which support and sustain their unique development.

In nurturing homes children know they are loved for themselves with all their beauty, their faults, their talents and their idiosyncrasies. They learn they are important because people love them, and not for how they look or what they do. They find that they can try things out and test themselves in safety, because it is all right to make mistakes and fail. They are taught they are special, because every human being is special, and not because they learn faster or slower than others, or do clever and surprising things. They learn they can expect to be treated fairly and with respect, and that they in turn have a responsibility towards others.

Nurturing classrooms and schools are environments in which children feel able to develop as fast and as far as they choose, and where they can display their talents naturally through all the activities they undertake. In nurturing classrooms children can ask challenging questions without fear of mockery and can be different without being treated as alien; learning is presented as exciting, and effort and achievement of all kinds are celebrated and rewarded. Nurturing schools organise activities which allow children to learn with and from each other, provide opportunities in school to compensate for what is not available in pupils' homes, keep a watchful eye on the climate in every classroom, and make clear the message that we achieve more together than on our own.

Behavioural checklists to help in the recognition of exceptional ability

Checklists, such as the one given here, are not tests to determine whether or not a particular child is exceptionally able. Each child is unique, and any one child may or may not show some, all or none of the characteristics described. But checklists can prove helpful in alerting parents and teachers to the possibility that they may be misjudging some of their children, and in encouraging them to look for positive signs of talents which they may have so far failed to acknowledge.

Many different checklists have been put forward, some fairly short and concise, others of great length and all-embracing detail. The one given below attempts to include the most commonly mentioned features, without becoming unnecessarily complex.

Exceptionally able children may show some of the following:

- Great intellectual curiosity; a desire to know the whys and the hows of all events; provocative and searching questions; dissatisfaction with simple explanations.

- Superior reasoning ability; ability to deal with abstract concepts, to generalise from specific facts, to see connections between events.

- Unusual persistence; a determination to complete tasks to their own satisfaction; ability to concentrate for long periods of time.

- Exceptional speed of thought, rapid response to new ideas.

- Ability to learn quickly and easily; understanding a task often before the full instructions or explanations have been given; needing little or no practice to acquire competence.

- Good memory; apparent lack of need to rehearse learning, or to revise.

- Extensive vocabulary; heightened sensitivity to language generally; insistence on the precise meaning of words; delight in technical terms.

- Acute powers of observation; close attention to detail.

- Vivid imagination, both verbally and in other creative work such as drawing and model-making.

- Divergent thinking; tendency to look for unusual ways of solving problems.

- Great initiative; preference for independent work.

- Highly developed sense of humour, often esoteric; delight in verbal puns.

- Unusually high personal standards; frustration if they cannot achieve the excellence they demand of themselves; perfectionist approach, not satisfied with approval from others.

- Impatience, both with self and with others; intolerance towards others less able than themselves; contempt for adults who talk down to them.

- Sensitivity and highly-strung behaviour; quick to react to disapproval; easily frustrated; highly perceptive.

- Wide range of interests; hobbies that are sometimes unusual and which are followed with great enthusiasm and competence; often keen collectors.

- Extensive knowledge and expertise in a particular subject.

- Preference for the company of older children and adults; boredom with the company and interests of peers.

- Desire to direct others in play and in group activities.

- Preoccupation with matters of philosophical and universal concern, such as the nature of man, the meaning of life, the concept of space, etc.

However, exceptionally able children may not necessarily show their talents in obvious or acceptable ways. They may for instance be:

- Unusually articulate, but unable to produce good or neatly written work.

- Restless, inattentive, given to daydreaming.

- Keen to get attention by playing the role of class clown.

- Reticent, or reluctant to demonstrate their knowledge or ability.

- Unwilling to follow instructions for class tasks, preferring to do things their own way.

- Unenthusiastic about classwork generally; appearing ungracious, uncooperative or apathetic.

- Hypercritical, persistently questioning the reasons given.

- Quick to note inconsistencies, to point out errors of logic or information.

- Uncomfortably forthright in their assessment of situations and in their ability to recognise discrepancies between what people think and what they do.

- Withdrawn; reluctant to take part in group tasks; appearing to prefer their own company.

None of these behaviours is proof of high ability, but they can alert adults to the need to question why the child is behaving in that way.

Bloom's Taxonomy

This hierarchy of knowledge, proposed by Benjamin Bloom in 1956, provides a useful structure for planning and evaluating different levels of challenge in the curriculum, and in individual tasks. Levels D,E,F are described as 'higher-order' skills.

Skills	Behaviour	Questions and activities
A. Knowledge	observation and recall, knowledge, mastery of subject matter...	list, define, tell, describe, identify, show, label, collect, examine, tabulate, quote, name...
B. Comprehension	understanding information, grasp meaning, translate knowledge into new context, interpret facts, compare, contrast, order, group, infer, predict...	summarise, describe, interpret, contrast, predict, associate, distinguish, differentiate, discuss, extend...
C. Application	use information, use methods, concepts, theories in new context, solve problems using relevant skills, knowledge...	apply, demonstrate, calculate, complete, illustrate, show, solve, examine, modify, relate, change, experiment...
D. Analysis	seeing patterns and organisation of parts, recognise hidden meanings, identify components...	analyse, separate, order, explain, connect, classify, arrange, divide, compare, select, explain, infer...

| E. Synthesis | use old ideas to create new ones, generalise from given facts, relate knowledge from several areas, predict, conclude... | combine, integrate, modify, rearrange, substitute, plan, create, design, invent, compose, formulate, prepare, generalise, rewrite. |
| F. Evaluation | compare and discriminate between ideas, assess value, make choices based on reasoned argument, verify, judge... | assess, rank, grade, test, measure, recommend, convince, select, judge, support, conclude, compare, summarise... |

Bibliography

References

Beck, J. (1968) *How to Raise a Brighter Child*. London: Souvenir Press.

Bloom, B. S. (1956) *Taxonomy of Education Objectives*. London: Methuen.

DfEE (1994) *Code of Practice on the Identification and Assessment of Special Educational Needs*. London: HMSO.

Deaux, K. and Emswiller, T. (1974) 'Explanations of Successful Performances on Sex-linked Tasks', *Journal of Personality and Social Psychology* **2**, 80-85.

Eyre, D. and Fuller, M. (1993) *Year 6 Teachers and More Able Pupils*. Oxford: National Primary Centre, Oxfordshire County Council.

Eyre, D. (1997) *Able Children in Ordinary Schools*. London: David Fulton Publishers.

Fisher, R. (1995) *Teaching Children to Think*. Cheltenham: Stanley Thornes Publishers.

Fox, L. H. and Zimmerman, W. (1985) 'Gifted Women', in Freeman, J. (ed.) *The Psychology of Gifted Children: Perspectives on Development and Education*. Chichester: Wiley.

Freeman, J. (1991) *Gifted Children Growing Up*. London: Cassell.

Freeman, J. (1991) *Bright as a Button*. London: Optima.

Freeman, J., Span, P., Wagner, H. (1995) *Actualizing Talent: A Lifelong Challenge*. London: Cassell.

Freeman, J. (1996) *Clever Children, Handbook for Parents*. London: Hamlyn Books.

Gardner, H. (1993) *Frames of Mind, The Theory of Multiple Intelligencies*, 2nd edn. London: Fontana/Collins.

George, D. (1997) *The Challenge of the Able Child*. London: David Fulton Publishers.

Heatherington, L. *et al.* (1989) 'Towards an understanding of the social consequences of feminine immodesty about personal achievement', *Sex Roles* **20**, 371–80.

Howe, M. J. A. (1996). Presentation to the British Psychological Society Annual Meeting, March 1996. Quoted in the *Observer*, 14 April 1996.

Kellmer Pringle, M. (1970) *Able Misfits: A Study of Educational and Behavioural Difficulties of 103 Very Intelligent Children.* London: Longman/National Children's Bureau.

Kelly, G. (1971) Chapter 1 in Bannister, D. and Fransella, F. *Inquiring Man, the Theory of Personal Constructs*, 11–43. London: Penguin.

Maslow, A. H. (1954) *Motivation and Personality.* New York: Harper.

Murray, L. (1997) Post-natal depression research findings quoted in the *Observer*, October.

Murris, K. (1992) *Teaching Philosophy with Picture Books.* London: Infonet Publications.

Norwich, B. (1996) 'Special needs education or education for all: connective specialism and idealogical impurity', in *British Journal of Special Education* **23** (3) 100–104.

Ogilive, E. (1973) *Gifted Children in Primary Schools.* Schools Council Research Studies. London: Macmillan.

Parkyn, G. W. (1948) *Children of High Intelligence, a New Zealand Study.* Oxford: Oxford University Press.

Schools Curriculum and Assessment Authority (SCAA) (1997) *Making Effective Use of Key Stage 2 Assessments.* Hayes: SCAA Publications.

Smith, A. (1996) *Accelerated Learning in the Classroom.* Stafford: Network Educational Press.

Storr, A. (1988) *The School of Genius.* London: Andre Deutsch.

Thomas, L. and Harri-Augstein, S. (1985) *Self-Organised Learning: Foundations of a conversational science for psychology.* London: Routledge and Kegan Paul.

Vail, P. (1979) *The World of the Gifted Child.* New York: Walker.

Walden, R. and Walkerdine, V. (1985) 'Girls and Mathematics: From Primary to Secondary Schooling', *Bedford Way Papers* **24**, London: Institute of Education, University of London.

Wall, W. D. (1968) *Adolescents in School and Society.* Slough: NFER.

Wood, D. (1988) *How Children Think and Learn.* Oxford: Blackwell.

Wood, D. (1993) 'The Classroom of 2015', *National Commission on Education: Briefing Paper 20.* London: Paul Hamlyn.

Further reading

Denton, C. and Postlethwaite, K. (1985) *Able Children: Identifying them in the Classroom*. Windsor: NFER/Nelson.

Eyre, D. and Marjoram, T. (1990) *Enriching and Extending the National Curriculum*. London: Kegan Paul.

Freeman, J. (1979) *Gifted Children: Their Identification and Development in a Social Context*. Lancaster: MTP Press.

Freeman, J.(1994) 'Some emotional aspects of being gifted', *Journal for the Education of the Gifted*, **17,** 180–97.

Harris, T. (1973) *I'm OK, You're OK*. London: Pan Books.

HMI. (1977) *Matters for Discussion: Gifted Children in Middle and Comprehensive Secondary Schools*. London: HMSO.

HMI. (1992) *Education Observed: The education of very able children in maintained schools*. London: HMSO.

Howe, M. J. A. (1990) *The Origins of Exceptional Abilities*. Oxford: Blackwell.

Hudson, L. (1966) *Contrary Imaginations*. London: Methuen.

Montgomery, D. (1996) *Educating the Able*. London: Cassell.

Quinn, V. (1997) *Critical Thinking in Young Minds*. London: David Fulton Publishers.

Stevens, A. (1980) *Clever Children in Comprehensive Schools*. Harmondsworth: Penguin.

Tempest, N. R. (1974) *Teaching Clever Children 7–11*. London and Boston: Routledge and Kegan Paul.

Vernon, P. E., Adamson, G., Vernon, D. (1977) *The Psychology and Education of Gifted Children*. London: Methuen.

Books which provide practical guidance for structuring and planning the curriculum

Bloom, B. S. (1956) *Taxonomy of Education Objectives*. London: Methuen.

Clarke, G. (1983) *Guidelines for the Recognition of Gifted Pupils*. London: Longman/Schools Council.

De Bono, E. (1976) *Teaching Thinking*. London: Temple-Smith.

Eyre, D. and Marjoram, T. (1990) *Enriching and Extending the National Curriculum*. London: Kegan Paul.

Eyre, D. (1997) *Able Children in Ordinary Schools*. London: David Fulton Publishers.

Evans, L. and Goodhew, G. (1997) *Providing for Able Children*. Dunstable: Folens Press.

Fisher, R. *et al.* (1987) *Problem Solving in Primary Schools*. Cheltenham: Stanley Thornes Publishers.

Fisher, R. (1995) *Teaching Children to Think*. Cheltenham: Stanley Thornes Publishers.

Fowler, W. F. (1990) *Talking from Infancy: How to nurture and cultivate Early Language Development*. Cambridge, MA: Brookline Books.

George, D. (1995) *Gifted Education: Identification and Provision*. London: David Fulton Publishers.

Kerry, T. (1981) *Teaching Bright Children*. London: Macmillan.

Kerry, T. (1982) *Effective Questioning*. London: Macmillan.

Murchinson, J. (1996) *Maths Problems for Gifted and Talented Students*. Colchester: Phoenix Education, Claire Publications and Jonothan Press.

Renzulli, J. S. (1977) *The Enrichment Triad Model: A Guide for Developing Defensible Programs for the Gifted and Talented*. Wethersfield, CT: Creative Learning Press.

Smith, A. (1996) *Accelerated Learning in the Classroom*. Stafford: Network Educational Press.

Teare, B. (1997) *Effective Provision for Able and Talented Children*. Stafford. Network Education Press.

Willings, D. (1980) *The Creatively Gifted: Recognising and Developing the Creative Personality*. Cambridge: Woodhead-Faulkner.

Wragg, E. R. (1993) *Questioning*. London: Routledge.

Useful sources of ideas and materials for activities at home and school

Beck, J. (1968) *How to Raise a Brighter Child*. London: Souvenir Press. (A compendium of creative ideas for parents for things to do with young children.)

De Bono, E. (1973) *Cort Thinking*. Direct Educational Services, 35 Albert St., Blandford, Dorset DT11 7HZ

De Bono, E. (1975) *Think Links*. Direct Educational Services, 35 Albert St., Blandford, Dorset DT11 7HZ

De Bono, E. (1992) *Teach Your Child How to Think*. Harmondsworth: Penguin. (A book for parents to encourage creative/lateral thinking.)

Chalkface Project Materials: *Enrichment Activities for More Able Students, 1, 2.* PO Box 1, Milton Keynes MK5 6JB (Useful range of activities for use in the classroom for individual pupils or small group work.)

Cheshire Management Guidelines: *Identifying and Providing for Our Most Able Pupils.* Cheshire County Council Education Services. (A very useful manual of guidance aimed at senior managers in schools, to help in school organisation and planning, covering: Definitions, Identification, Interventions, Management, Contact addresses. The model formats for planning and recording, and for a whole-school policy are likely to be especially helpful.)

Dickinson, C. (1996) *Effective Learning Activities.* Stafford: Network Educational Press. (Second title in a series of handbooks which provide practical ideas for raising pupil achievement. It shows how teachers can plan activities which challenge able children as well as support the less able within the current curriculum structures.)

Fisher, R. Occasional Papers: including *Teaching Thinking; Creative Thinking; Questioning for Thinking; Moral Education; The Thinking Child; Stories for Thinking.* The Centre for Thinking Skills, West London Institute, 300 St Margaret's Road, Twickenham, London SW1 1BT (A series of booklets with both theoretical discussion and practical examples for activities to promote effective thinking strategies.)

Freeman, J. (1983) *Clever Children – Handbook for Parents.* London: Hamlyn.

Jackson, B. (1980) *Your Exceptional Child.* London: Fontana.

Lake, M. (1991) *Brill the Brave.* Birmingham: Questions Publishing. (Stories used as the basis for philosophical enquiry in the Primary Thinking Skills Project.)

Smith, A. (1996) *Accelerated Learning in the Classroom,* Stafford: Network Educational Press. (First book in an excellent series of practical handbooks to help schools raise achievement. It shows how teachers can translate theories about learning into practical activities which increase motivation and raise pupil attainment.)

Organisations

Centre for Philosophy for Children. Details: K. Morris, University of Wales College, Swansea. SA2 8PP. Courses, information and materials on philosophy for children.

Centre for Thinking Skills. Details: R. Fisher, West London Institute, 300 St Margaret's Road, Twickenham TW1 1PT. Booklets and resources for teaching thinking.

NACE: National Association for Able Children in Education. Westminster College, Oxford OX2 9AT. The main centre for information and support for teachers and parents. Membership of NACE is open to individuals and organisations. The centre publishes regular newletters and a twice-yearly publication, *Flying High*.

CHI: Children of High Intelligence. PO Box 4222, London SE22 8XG. A support society which organises activities for able children and their families in different parts of the country.

National Association for Gifted Children (NAGC). A registered charity which organises activities, arranges meetings and advises parents.

LEA Educational Psychology Services. Educational psychologists working with the local authority services offer advice, counselling and support to both children and their families. Parents can usually make contact either directly or through their child's school.

Index

DATE DUE

JUL 1 0 2000		
JAN 1 5 2002		

Demco, Inc. 38-293